Teaching Grammar: From Rules to Reasons

Danny Norrington-Davies

Teaching Grammar: From Rules to Reasons

Practical ideas and advice for working with grammar in the language classroom

© Danny Norrington-Davies

The author has asserted his rights in accordance with the Copyright, Designs and Patents Act (1988) to be identified as the author of this work.

Published by:

Pavilion Publishing and Media Ltd
Rayford House
School Road
Hove, East Sussex
BN3 5HX

Tel: 01273 434 943
Fax: 01273 227 308
Email: info@pavpub.com

First published 2016.

A catalogue record for this book is available from the British Library.

ISBNs: 978-1-911028-22-2

Pavilion is the leading training and development provider and publisher in the health, social care and allied fields, providing a range of innovative training solutions underpinned by sound research and professional values. We aim to put our customers first, through excellent customer service and value.

Author: Danny Norrington-Davies
Production editor: Mike Benge, Pavilion Publishing and Media Ltd
Cover design: Phil Morash, Pavilion Publishing and Media Ltd
Page layout and typesetting: Emma Dawe, Pavilion Publishing and Media Ltd
Printer: CPI UK

Teaching Grammar:
From Rules to Reasons

Teaching Grammar: From Rules to Reasons

Also available from Pavilion Publishing and Media

ETpedia	ISBN 978-1-910366-13-4
Become an Online English Teacher	ISBN 978-1-910366-77-6
Teaching English One to One	ISBN 978-1-898789-12-3
Teaching English with Drama	ISBN 978-1-898789-11-6
Teaching English with Information Technology	ISBN 978-1-898789-16-1

For full details of all our books and our range of magazines for teachers and students, including:

English Teaching Professional

Modern English Teacher

visit: **www.etprofessional.com**

www.modernenglishteacher.com

Contents

About the author

Danny Norrington-Davies is a teacher and teacher trainer. He began teaching in 1993 in Botswana and now works at International House in London.
As a language teacher, his interests are grammar, materials development, emerging language, critical thinking and visualisation, and he is a member of the C Group, an independent and informal grouping of ELT professionals. It aims collaboratively to share information, promote reflection and enquiry, and encourage action through more creative teaching practices. Danny also enjoys attending and speaking at conferences, and has published articles for *The Teacher Trainer, Folio* and *HLT magazine*. This is his first book.

Introduction

I am fascinated by English grammar and enjoy teaching it, but this wasn't always the case. In fact, when I first started teaching back in 1993, I worried about grammar and most of my planning time was spent learning about rules, anticipating problems and working out ways of helping my students understand what I was trying to teach them. Even with the hours spent studying and preparing, I still worried that I would make a mistake or struggle to answer my students' questions.

So what changed? The first development was learning that I enjoyed working things out with my students, so that rather than seeing their questions as problems I had to solve, I was able to view them as opportunities for discovery and learning. The second development came when I began to question the knowledge I had gained from grammars, teaching materials and coursebooks and started to look at grammar in a different way. This led me to try out a new way of working with grammar in the classroom, which ultimately led me to write this book.

This is a book about grammar and grammar teaching, but more than that, it is a book about what speakers and writers of English do with grammar and how language students can be guided to discover meaning. As such, this book provides an alternative view of grammar to those found in coursebooks, grammars or other published sources, and outlines an alternative approach to teaching grammar in the language classroom. In addition, this book will help you develop your knowledge of grammar, provide a source of grammar lessons and give you new ways of planning and organising lessons. I hope this book can also help you develop the same fascination with grammar that I have.

How the book is organised

This book is divided into three sections.

Section 1 is both theoretical and practical. Chapter 1 looks at the reasons why it is important to teach grammar in the language classroom and explores ways in which this can be done. Chapter 2 examines the use of pedagogic grammar rules, before chapter 3 introduces an innovative way of exploring grammar in the language classroom.

Section 2 is practical. Part 1 contains 18 text- and task-based lessons that can be used in class at a variety of levels. This part also includes tips for practising teachers, examples of student work, overviews of various classroom approaches and suggestions on how teachers can work with learner language. Part 2 contains guidance on designing lessons and creating your own materials. This will be useful for new and experienced teachers as well as teacher developers working on training courses.

Section 3 concludes the book by answering questions arising from the contents of the previous chapters and explores how the approach outlined in the book can be adapted to suit different teaching contexts.

In this book, you will also see that some of the learner-generated reasons are grammatically inaccurate. These are indicated with the symbol †. When you get to these, consider how you might reformulate them. Where an error is particularly complicated, interesting or open to interpretation, suggestions for reformulations can be found in the teacher's notes starting on page 181. These are indicated with the symbol ††.

A note about the terminology used in the book

This book outlines an alternative way of teaching grammar in the language classroom and includes examples of how this works in practice. During this discussion, the author regularly uses the term *approach*. This word is used in a broad sense to describe classroom procedures, practices, techniques and activities rather than the theory or principles that inform a teaching method.

Acknowledgements

The author would like to thank the following people: Evadne Adrian-Vallance for her editorial support and guidance; Fiona Richmond, Helena Gomm, Chia Suan Chong, Mike Benge and the team at Pavilion Publishing; Maureen McGarvey for all her encouragement and support; Catriona

Johnson for introducing me to transposition; Will Morrow for his sketches; colleagues at International House, London, for all their support and inspiration; finally, the students who influenced the content of this book by looking at grammar differently.

For Gemma with love

Section 1

1. Why focus on grammar in the language classroom?

'A funny thing happens to grammar in the classroom.'
Donald Freeman

Introduction

If you gathered together a varied group of language teachers and asked them to choose a list of issues they wanted to discuss, it would be surprising if the subject of grammar did not come up fairly quickly. After all, it is possible that nothing has divided teachers' beliefs and practices over the years as much as the importance of grammar and how it should be taught in the language classroom (Thornbury, 1999).

This chapter:

- looks at the development of Communicative Language Teaching and the shift from grammar to communication
- discusses the reasons why a focus on grammar is an important part of Communicative Language Teaching methodology
- examines teachers' attitudes to grammar and grammar teaching
- explores different approaches and techniques that can be used to balance grammar work with communicative practice.

The development of Communicative Language Teaching

In the 1970s, most language teaching syllabuses were organised in terms of grammatical structures, and courses generally consisted of a progression of discrete grammatical items that students were expected to master one after the other (Wilkins, 1976). The standard approach was a deductive one, and the key features of what was considered to be good teaching practice were the presentation of grammatical rules, extensive pronunciation drills and controlled practice exercises. The main emphasis, therefore, was on accurate use of grammatical items and correct pronunciation. However, important reforms were underway that began to shift the priority of language teaching away from these goals, towards more genuine language use in real-life situations (Howatt & Smith, 2014).

So what drove these reforms? First, it was increasingly felt that a focus on structure alone was inadequate for learning, as it did not help students to use the target language to communicate in real-life situations. At the heart of this idea were academics and sociolinguists such as J. L. Austin, Henry Widdowson and Del Hymes, who argued that the primary purpose of language is to communicate. Therefore, one of the main goals of language teachers is to provide students with the tools to do so more naturally and effectively.

Further reforms were prompted by the Council of Europe project of 1971, which set out to create comprehensive guidelines for syllabuses, the design of teaching and learning materials and the assessment of foreign language proficiency. Now known as the CEFR (the Common European Framework of Reference for Languages), the project posed two important questions: 1) What will learners need to do with the target language? 2) What will they need to learn in order to achieve those ends? (Council of Europe, 2002). This project, along with the first lists or inventories of core topics, situations, skills and functions, led to the creation of syllabuses and coursebooks that contained more practical or functional aims than structural ones.

At the same time, a school of thought was developing that argued that language awareness was not even necessary for acquisition. In fact, it was suggested that an overt focus on the form of the language was the cause of a lot of ineffective language teaching and unsuccessful learning. This belief was fuelled by the work of Tracy Terrell, Stephen Krashen and N. S. Prabhu, who each suggested that language proficiency could not be formally taught and learnt. They argued instead that it was acquired naturally. Despite differences in their methodologies, all three questioned the need for an explicit focus on grammar, either through explanations, rule discovery or focused error correction, and their ideas were to have a significant and lasting impact on the way that languages were taught in the L2 classroom.

First, Terrell and Krashen claimed that for language acquisition to take place all that is required is a sufficient amount of comprehensible input. In other words, if students are exposed to enough language that is slightly above their current level of proficiency, acquisition will naturally take place. The teacher's role therefore is simply to provide the right amount of input and to help learners with comprehension. Prabhu, meanwhile, suggested that language learning takes place when students are given opportunities to communicate in the L2. He consequently created a syllabus in which the objective of each lesson was the completion of a communicative task rather than the successful use of a specific grammar structure. This syllabus, known as the Bangalore Project, was a strong version of an approach that has come to be known as Task-based Learning (TBL) or Task-based Language Teaching (TBLT).

So over a short period of time, a number of ideas and beliefs had emerged that challenged the value of structural syllabuses, the teaching of discrete grammatical items and the mechanical practice of language patterns. The resulting new models of teaching came to be labelled as Communicative Language Teaching (CLT), which had as its heart the basic principle that students should be given opportunities for authentic and meaningful language use through communicative activities and tasks. This model of teaching rapidly became extremely popular, and for some time after the emergence of CLT, the status of grammar became uncertain (Nunan, 1989). Its role was questioned further as greater understanding of the lexical system was gained. This knowledge led to calls to shift the emphasis of language instruction from the study of grammar and grammar rules to a focus on lexis and prefabricated chunks of language (eg. Widdowson, 1990; Lewis, 1993).

Why focus on grammar in the communicative language classroom?

Although a zero grammar approach was accepted in some quarters, the idea that CLT is or ever was anti-grammar is a bit of a misconception. In fact, the basic but broad principle of 'learning through doing' that was the foundation of much CLT methodology means that there have always been different interpretations of how CLT can be applied in the classroom (Dörnyei, 2009).

On the one hand, some teachers and methodologists recommend what Thornbury (1999) calls a 'deep-end' approach to CLT, in which there is no overt focus on grammar. A great number of teachers, however, call for more of a 'shallow-end' approach, which gives attention to both functional and structural aspects of the language in order to help learners complete communicative tasks more successfully. In other words, grammar awareness is seen as a way of helping learners communicate rather than the goal itself. So in what ways does grammar teaching help?

1. Grammar enables you to create an infinite number of sentences

It's important to have these mechanisms and formulas to help you find out how things work so that you can then apply them in other situations. A lot of people think it's a boring and laborious thing that's hard to do, but it's a useful tool. It's a structure to build communication on.

David (Teaches English to adults, UK)

Because the grammatical system of a language enables speakers and writers to create an infinite variety of messages and meanings, it is impossible to use language creatively without it (Littlewood, 1985). In this regard, grammar can be seen as a kind of 'sentence-making machine' (Thornbury, 1999), though I prefer the term 'meaning-making machine', which enables learners to express themselves in a variety of different situations.

However, learning grammatical patterns is clearly not enough. Students also need to acquire a good range of lexis and formulaic expressions in order to communicate their message clearly and without a great deal of effort (Lewis, 1993). In addition, creating accurate sentences must not be the main goal of instruction, as this ability will be of little use if students are not able to take part in genuinely communicative situations. It is for this reason that grammar items should not merely be presented one after the other and then practised at sentence level. Instead, they need to be looked at in meaningful contexts and learners must be given opportunities to generate patterns during genuine communicative interactions.

2. Grammatical input helps learners fine-tune what they want to say

Grammar helps us refine our language. In class I try to help my students rebuild unclear English sentences with grammar and to give lots of practice. **Kyong Sook (High school teacher, South Korea)**

Targeted grammatical input can help L2 learners avoid miscommunication and add depth and subtlety to the meanings they want to express (Thornbury, 1999). Though it is possible to communicate very efficiently with lexis alone, and teachers should not insist on correct grammar purely for the sake of it, there will come a time when students need grammar to convey their message more clearly and to avoid potential misunderstandings. Take the following example:

I am study here for two months †

Though this student's use of lexis gives a lot of clues as to the meaning, the message is not entirely clear. Has this student been studying for two months already or are they at the beginning of a two month course? Even if the student has just been asked how long they are studying for, this answer could still be unclear to a teacher who has just taken over the class or to a student who has just joined. Therefore, this learner needs some grammatical input to help them see how they can express this particular idea more clearly, for example:

I've been studying here for two months.
or
I'm studying here for two months.

 In other words, grammar would help the student fine-tune what they wanted to say so that their message was clear. Seen from this perspective, grammar is not an optional add-on; it lies at the very heart of effective communication (Lock, 1996).

It is not just teachers and methodologists who believe it is important to help learners refine what they want to say. Many students also have a strong desire to express themselves clearly, and some will struggle to move on until they can do so. This can be seen in the following exchange, in which two students, talking about their aims and plans for the future, are unable to get past the fact that they cannot find the most effective way of saying what they want to say. This is despite the fact that S2 understands the meaning that S1 is trying to express. Targeted correction or guidance would enable them to get past this block and help them convey their meaning precisely.

S1: I'll be quitting smoking (pause) no …

S2: No?

S1: No.

S2: No what?

S1: Not 'I'll be quitting smoking'.

S2: No.

S1: Will be …

S2: … will be quit …

S1: …will be quitted …

(long pause)

S2: You will be quit … (nodding)

(long pause)

S1: You understand?

S2: Yeah, you will be quit.

S1: I will be quit.

(long pause)

S1: (to self) is not that …

3. A focus on grammar can prevent fossilisation

I learnt French in a very immersive way and I can't correct the mistakes that I learnt when I was in school. So I'm kind of stuck with it. I'm quite a good communicator but I'm actually making all these mistakes. So I think the grammar is an important thing to get right at those early stages so the mistakes don't follow you. **Tanya (Trainee on a CELTA course, UK)**

Michael Long (1991) suggests that a failure to include a focus on language in communicative practice can result in fossilisation, the process by which an L2 error becomes a permanent part of a learner's language. He also claims that without input, students will fail to make much progress beyond the initial success they experience when they first start learning. He therefore argues that errors made during communicative tasks should be picked up and corrected in feedback stages. This enables learners to notice the difference between the error and the correct version within the context of what they want to say, which makes any language input that follows far more meaningful and useful. Long argues that this type of feedback, which he labels 'Focus on Form', is a necessary element of language teaching and learning. Without it, students may find themselves in the same position as Tanya, whose experience as a language learner has clearly informed one of her teaching beliefs.

4. Grammar can help students use lexis more effectively

I prefer focusing on lexis and the grammar that comes with that. From experience as a teacher and language learner, you can communicate with the right words even if your grammar is terrible. **Ayan (General English teacher, UK)**

Henry Widdowson (1990), one of the leading figures in CLT, suggests that a natural and effective approach to language instruction would be to make lexis the starting point. However, this does not mean that grammar is removed from teaching syllabuses altogether. Instead, students are introduced to lexical items first, then shown how they work grammatically. This approach creates a different type of meaning-making machine.

How does this work in practice? Let us take the semantically related words *expel, release, discharge* and *check out* (drawn from McCarthy *et al*, 2010). When learning these items, it is important that students know which other words they typically occur with and which ones they do not. In other words, students need to learn the most frequent and common collocations. For example,

expel + school

release + prison

discharge + hospital

check out + hotel

~~*expel + hotel*~~

~~*check out + school*~~

As well as exploring collocations, it is also important to show learners how these words are typically used together in grammatical patterns. This is known as colligation. Have a look at the examples below. What are the differences between the first three verbs and the last one?

He was expelled from school.

He was released from prison.

He was discharged from hospital.

He checked out of the hotel.

Firstly, *check out* is active whereas the first three examples are all passive. By raising awareness of this pattern, students will be able to understand that *check out* is an action that is performed by the speaker, whereas the other three verbs all signify actions that are done by somebody else to the speaker. This does not mean that none of the other three verbs can be used in an active sentence. Corpus research shows that they can, but with *expel* and *release* this happens very infrequently. In addition, when they are used in active sentences, a reflexive pronoun (eg. *himself*) needs to be used. This changes the grammatical pattern:

He discharged himself from hospital.

He released himself gently.

It is also useful to demonstrate to students that where certain words are related by sense or meaning, the grammatical patterns they occur in can be similar. For example, the verbs of perception *see, hear and watch* are frequently followed by an object + either the base form of a verb or the *-ing* form:

> *I heard them leave / leaving.*
> *Didn't you see me signal / signalling?*
> *We watched it fall / falling.*

In fact, it would be logical to assume that words related by meaning would behave in the same way, as *select* and *choose* do below (drawn from Lackman, 2016).

> *She was chosen to represent her country.*
> *(subject + choose (passive) + infinitive)*
>
> *She was selected to represent her country.*
> *(subject + selected (passive) + infinitive)*

However, this is not always the case. Corpus research has shown that where *choose* and *select* can both be followed by the infinitive in a passive sentence, the same is not always true of active sentences, where *select* is very rarely used.

> *We chose to go by train. (subject + choose + infinitive)*
> *We selected to go by train.*

These are all useful areas to explore, and looking at language in this way has a number of advantages: 1) it helps students to build on the lexis they learn so they can communicate more effectively; 2) it demonstrates to students that words occur with other words in specific grammatical patterns; 3) it raises awareness and understanding of the English grammatical system while inputting a sufficient range of lexis. It also lends weight to the idea that grammar and vocabulary are both taught more effectively in combination (Dellar & Walkley, 2016).

5. Grammar can be interesting for students

When a learner is aware of how their own language works because they are naturally interested in this area, they find grammar explanations useful, as they can compare, contrast and analyze L1 and L2 structures. The same is true when a learner already knows a second language.
Mercedes (English teacher and teacher trainer, Argentina)

A lot of new teachers or those on training courses have concerns about teaching grammar in class, worrying that it will be boring or difficult for students. However, it is not really the grammar itself that is dull. It is more likely to be the methods used by the teacher or the teaching materials. Exploring grammar in meaningful and engaging contexts and giving students time and space to work things out for themselves can be extremely stimulating and motivating. In addition, working collaboratively with other students in hypothesising about rules, uses and meanings is useful communicative practice in its own right. As Ellis (2002b) suggests, talking about grammar might even be more meaningful than talking about some general topics often found in teaching materials and communicative language courses.

6. Some students want to focus on grammar

When I was learning Spanish, I always wanted to know *why* and I couldn't move beyond a certain piece of language until I knew why. I therefore think you need that structure. I think it's very important.
Azka (Trainee teacher on a CELTA course, Pakistan)

Although many teachers believe that students expect to learn about grammar because this is what they experienced in previous classes, this is not the reason why all students want to study grammar. In fact, some learners come to classes specifically for a more structured focus on language than they have previously had, or for the chance to receive some corrective feedback. This is especially the case for students who have experienced frustration while trying to learn a language outside the classroom or those who have only had access to conversation classes. Teachers who then ignore this need by taking a zero grammar approach are likely to frustrate and alienate this type of student during their courses (Thornbury, 1999).

As can be seen from Azka's comment above, some students also want to understand why things are the way they are. This is common for many adult learners, who are reluctant to move on to practice until they understand what certain structures mean or when they will need to use them. As a language learner myself, this is something I can relate to.

7. Some students need to focus on grammar

I believe students need communicative skills more than grammar, but since we have to follow a syllabus set by the Ministry of Education, we have to follow the book, and it is generally related to grammar. The students will also have to pass a test that is mainly focused on grammar.
Ece (High school teacher, Cyprus)

For many teachers, grammar is an important part of the syllabus. Because their students need to understand and manipulate specific grammatical structures in order to pass tests or exams, an explicit focus on language items is therefore expected. Where time is also limited, or for teachers who work with particularly large classes, this can mean that explicit teacher-fronted explanations are the quickest and most 'efficient' ways of helping the student.

Although this kind of deductive approach goes against many teachers' beliefs about what constitutes effective language teaching, it is important to consider the immediate needs of the learners and the situation they find themselves in. It is also important to recognise that this kind of teaching can have an effect, as Jun attests to below.

I didn't learn speaking, listening or writing when I was in high school. The only thing I learnt in my classes was grammar. But when I graduated from high school and started studying at university I needed to read a textbook written in English and learning grammar was very helpful because I could understand the textbook. Grammar built up some concrete ideas about how to make sentences in English. So when I looked at English sentences, I could understand. **Jun (High school teacher, South Korea)**

8. Grammar input lays the foundations for future learning

Ellis (2002a) argues that explicit grammar teaching does aid L2 language acquisition, but that it has a delayed rather than an immediate effect. In other words, language input does not enable students to use a particular form naturally and unconsciously straightaway. Instead, it is part of a longer process. First, learners need to become aware of the new language and understand what it means. This understanding then primes them to notice the same structure in future input, which helps them acquire the form when they are developmentally ready to do so.

Richard Schmidt (1990) makes strong claims about the value of noticing, suggesting that L2 learners cannot begin to acquire a language item or use it automatically until they have become consciously aware of it during input. Drawing on his experience of learning Portuguese in Brazil, Schmidt found that when he was interacting with local people, the language items that caught his attention tended to be the ones he had studied in his language classes, and though he was not able to use these structures automatically, something had stuck with him. He therefore suggested that one role of the teacher is to draw students' attention to structures that might otherwise escape their notice. This would help learners recognise these items later on, which would indirectly influence their future learning.

Schmidt also claims that learners need to 'notice the gap' between what they are able to do when using the target language and how the language is used in the input. In other words, if students notice that they cannot do something, or they recognise a difference between their L1 and the L2, this knowledge can help them develop the skills and the language awareness to use a particular language item more effectively in the future. As Nora suggests below, comparison between the L1 and L2 can be a useful tool for helping learners notice differences and similarities.

> When I was learning English, I used to focus so much on how English language is structured. I would compare it to L1 in order to understand the differences and the similarities before producing it. Years later when I started teaching, my EFL students reacted in a similar way and I concluded that it is a natural process for the human brain to look for a reference to something it is familiar with before it is able to accept a new form of language and to use it.
> **Nora (Teacher trainer, Algeria)**

Communicative tasks also play a key role, as these will provide further opportunities for students to notice gaps. In order to maximise the value of communicative tasks, Swain (1985) suggests that learners need to be pushed so that they are made to communicate in challenging or unfamiliar situations, as learning occurs when speakers encounter difficulties while communicating. By becoming aware that they are struggling to express themselves, the learner is primed to notice a gap. By then reflecting on the experience, the student can learn something new about the language. Because they are also getting opportunities to communicate in real time, this may eventually help them develop fluency.

Grammar teaching techniques in CLT

As seen above, there are a number of reasons why it is important to include a focus on grammar in the language classroom, and there is now compelling evidence to suggest that a combination of language-focused and meaning-focused learning leads to greater success for students than a focus on only one or the other (Spada, 2015). It is unlikely that any of the grammar we teach will truly stick unless students are given frequent opportunities to notice it and to put it to use in genuinely communicative tasks (Thornbury, 2004). Recent research suggests that this is the view of the majority of teachers (eg. Borg & Burns, 2008) and that students also see great value in grammar instruction being linked to real-life activities (eg. Loewen *et al*, 2009). Although grammar teaching has remained quite traditional in many parts of the world, communication and meaningful interaction have become central principles of many language classes and courses, and corrective feedback and activities that help learners 'notice the gap' have also become extremely common. These principles have led to the creation of a range of activities and approaches that enable teachers to balance meaning-based or communicative tasks with an explicit focus on language.

1. Noticing and consciousness-raising tasks through texts

By highlighting specific forms in a range of different text types, learners can be helped to understand how a grammatical item is structured, how it is used and why. Although the long-term impact of noticing may be delayed, it can prepare students for future input or help them to incorporate the item in follow-up communicative tasks. Teachers can also help students to develop noticing strategies away from the classroom so that they can begin to use the skill independently and autonomously (Thornbury, 1997b). This then enables learners to build their conscious knowledge and understanding of how the language works or how it is used socially and culturally. In addition, exposing students to a wide range of texts provides the type of input that Krashen (1982) suggests is necessary for acquisition to occur.

2. Rule-discovery activities

Another type of consciousness-raising task, rule-discovery activities help learners to develop explicit knowledge about grammar. However, rather than merely helping students to notice a grammatical item in the input, rule-discovery activities encourage learners to formulate a rule for how it is structured and how it is used. While language-focused stages can be done deductively (ie. students are presented with the rule) most of the evidence suggests that an inductive or discovery approach is a more effective way of enabling students to understand rules (Brown, 2007). This subsequently helps them to incorporate items of language into communicative tasks or to understand examples in texts more efficiently. Like noticing, it can also prime students for further hypothesising in the future, thereby directly influencing their learning and language development.

3. Pre-task planning and preparation stages

Before taking part in communicative tasks, a planning stage can help students to fine-tune their performance by giving them time to think about what they want to say and how they are going to say it. It can also help students to use a wider range of language than they might otherwise do during more spontaneous interactions (Ortega, 2005). To help them prepare for communicative tasks, students can use dictionaries, consult corpora, ask questions, make notes or even rehearse what they want to say with a partner or teacher. In addition, model texts can be used to help students notice examples of language that they can incorporate in the task or to show them how proficient speakers use language to complete the task.

During preparation stages, teachers act as advisors, building learners' confidence, helping them notice gaps and upgrading the language they use to perform the task. The advantage of this type of focus on form is that the meaning and function of what the learner wants to say is already clear, which means that the teacher does not need to go into a complex explanation of meaning. It is also possible that because there is an immediate need for the language item, the learner is more developmentally ready to learn it (Long & Norris, 2009).

4. The use of communicative tasks and student–student interaction

Communicative tasks enable students to use language to tell stories, share information, express opinions, propose ideas and solve problems. In the process, learners do not just get the opportunity to use the target language naturally and creatively; they are also able to think about their language use and to modify it and learn from it. This is one of the reasons that communication and student–student interaction form the basis of some contemporary approaches, such as TBL and Dogme, or play an important part in others, for example, the third stage of a PPP lesson (present-practice-produce), one of the most popular and durable lesson shapes in use today (Anderson, 2016).

5. Corrective feedback after communicative tasks

By recasting or reformulating learner language after or during communicative tasks, the teacher helps learners to notice the gaps between what they have tried to say and an appropriate or more acceptable way of saying it. Because the language input is provided when meaning is most salient, the learner is more likely to understand than if the language point was presented in isolation. As in preparation stages, they are subsequently more likely to be ready to learn it.

6. Grammaticisation tasks

Corrective feedback does not only need to be done after communicative tasks. It can also be done during or after learners perform grammaticisation tasks such as dictogloss, text reconstructions or writing a story based on a set of pictures. Another grammaticisation task is one where learners are provided with words that they must combine and add grammar to in order to create a complete, coherent and grammatically accurate stretch of language, as can be seen in the exercise below. As the students do the task, the teacher monitors and provides feedback that focuses on the difference between the learners' version and the original model.

> **Use the words below to write a complete introduction to this newspaper article.**
>
> Two men from North England arrest after attempt bring rare and protect animal species into country via London airport.

Unlike more controlled grammar practice activities such as gap-fills, grammaticisation tasks such as this have the value of being more open-ended. This is because students are able to come up with different answers and interpretations, which can then be explored or corrected in feedback:

> 1. Two men from the North of England were arrested after they attempted to bring rare and protected animal species into the country.
> 2. Two men from Northern England were arrested after attempting to bring rare, protected animal species into the country.
> 3. Two men from the North of England were arrested after attempting to bringing rare and protected animal species into the country. †

Grammaticisation tasks have a number of other advantages. First, the students are encouraged to think about and discuss how they can use grammar to make the text more coherent and whole. In this regard, the process of doing the task is as important as the outcome. The feedback then enables students to notice how well they are using grammar to create coherent messages and to compare the difference between their version and those of another set of students. In addition, this shift from lexis to grammar mirrors the way we develop our first language and how we are thought to initially start to pick up a second language. Finally, grammaticisation tasks can help students to see that grammar is not a constraint but a 'liberating force', helping people to express themselves with more than just words (Widdowson, 1990).

Each of these activities and techniques is aimed at making grammar forms salient to learners at or around the point that they need them, and by using texts, tasks and grammaticisation activities, this is always achieved in meaning-focused stages. With further exposure and practice, it is more likely that they will then be able to use the new language more effectively or spontaneously in the future.

Conclusion

Grammar plays an important role in the language learning process, but grammar knowledge must not be the single goal of instruction. Instead, it needs to be taught so that it helps students achieve better comprehension and enables them to communicate more effectively in genuine interactions. With these being the primary aims in the communicative language classroom, CLT can be seen as a broad collection of ideas that have come to be accepted as 'good practice' by many contemporary teachers (Mitchell, 1994). These ideas include:

- a greater emphasis on language as an aid to developing communication skills

- the use of more inductive, discovery approaches

- more student–student negotiation about language and meaning through pair and group work

- the use of texts and more authentic materials to raise learner awareness about language

- a greater focus on learner language and corrective feedback

- increased emphasis on strategies and learner autonomy.

It would seem that there are compelling reasons for studying grammar in the language classroom, and teachers can call on a range of effective approaches and techniques for doing so. However, there is an issue with both the way that grammar is described and how it is presented in a lot of contemporary coursebooks and teaching materials, and this idea will now be explored in the next chapter.

2. The use of grammar rules

'We try to contain the language with rules but the language runs away.'
Andrea Borsato

Introduction

Chapter 1 explored the reasons why it is beneficial for L2 learners to consciously focus on grammar in the language classroom, and it discussed a range of different approaches and techniques for doing so. This chapter looks at descriptions of language and, in particular, the use of pedagogic grammar rules. These are rules that are designed for students learning about the structure of their own language but have long been considered suitable for L2 language instruction, as in the following examples:

- State verbs are not usually used in progressive forms.
- The definite article is used when the listener or reader knows or can work out which particular person or thing we are talking about.
- Use the past progressive to describe an action in progress at a specific time in the past.
- The passive is used when the doer is not known or not important.
- *Used to* describes habits and repeated actions that took place over a period of time but have usually stopped.

This chapter also:

- provides a brief history of grammars and grammar rules
- discusses the pros and cons of using such rules in the classroom and in our teaching materials
- explores the way that rules are commonly described in coursebooks, teaching materials and grammars
- questions whether rules should be rejected altogether.

A brief history of grammar rules

Despite the size and challenge of the undertaking, linguists, scholars, academics and teachers have been creating grammars and descriptions of language rules from as long ago as the 6th century BC, when the first grammars of Sanskrit are said to have been written, while William Bullokar's *Bref Grammar for English*, published in 1586, is considered to mark the beginning of the English grammar tradition (Dons, 2004).

Because early English grammars were mostly based on Latin or sometimes Greek grammars, they are known as 'traditional grammars', and until the middle of the 19th century, they had an enormous influence on the way that English was taught in schools. Indeed, they still influence some of today's grammars in that many of the rules for syntax are drawn from Latin, often inappropriately, and Latinate terms are used to describe word class. Traditional grammars also attempt to state how a language *ought* to be used rather than how it *is* used, and because of this, they are also known as 'prescriptive grammars'. In a prescriptive grammar, formal written language is thought to be superior to informal and spoken varieties, and prescriptive grammarians also believe that rules cannot be broken. As such, some language is considered non-standard and therefore incorrect, despite the fact that the global spread of English has meant that it is inaccurate to say that it is still characterised by one uniform standard.

Though Crystal (2003) believes that today's grammarians are 'the inheritors of the distortions and limitations imposed by two centuries of a Latinate perspective', grammars have actually evolved rapidly over recent decades as linguists have been able to draw on large bodies of spoken and written texts, or corpora, to better understand how speakers and writers use language. This has resulted in today's more comprehensive descriptive grammars, which unlike prescriptive grammars, attempt to describe the language as it *is* used rather than to state how it ought to be used. However, the huge amount of data available to today's linguists presents its own set of challenges.

Thompson (2004) emphasises the extent of this challenge when he says that 'the meanings that we want to express, or the uses to which we may want to put language, are clearly messy: they appear so varied and so dependent on the infinite range of different contexts that it is difficult at first to see how we might impose order on them'. Moreover, the challenge of creating a comprehensive descriptive grammar is only becoming more demanding because even as you read this, 'the English language is changing, morphing, fragmenting and merging [and] no single "grammar" is capable of capturing this dynamism and complexity' (Thornbury, 2015). Unsurprisingly in the light of Thornbury's claims about the way that English is changing and growing, Bullokar's original grammar is dwarfed by today's reference grammars, some of which can contain close to 2,000 pages (eg. Huddlestone & Pullum, 2002).

For the purposes of this book we will look mainly at the issues with pedagogic grammar rules, as these are the ones that are most commonly used for L2 language instruction. This has meant that they have found their way into a vast collection of language teaching coursebooks, materials and syllabuses, where grammar points and rules are often organised according to their usefulness and supposed ease of learning. In fact, Thornbury (2015) suggests that coursebook grammar can even be viewed as a subset of pedagogic grammar, though one with a particularly narrow focus. Perhaps the most well-known and successful example of a pedagogic grammar that serves many of the same functions as a coursebook is Raymond Murphy's (2012) *English Grammar in Use*, now in its fourth edition.

However, because pedagogic or coursebook grammar rules are often too general or are taken from sentence level examples with little context, the meanings and uses described are often different to the rules found in descriptive grammars. Descriptive grammars are far more extensive than pedagogic grammars and show how language is used in modern life, covering both spoken and written examples as well as formal and informal language. Therefore, when L2 learners read and listen to authentic texts or are involved in genuine communicative tasks, they will be exposed to examples of language use that would be included in a descriptive grammar but might contradict the simplified rules found in a pedagogic grammar or the coursebooks they have been using. This presents a problem both for L2 learners and for teachers, as we will shortly see.

The value of rules

It is true that rules can play an important role in the language classroom. To begin with, clear and simple rules are a psychological comfort for learners and novice or newly qualified teachers, providing both with the feeling that they can understand and have some control over the very complex material they are faced with learning and teaching. As Larsen-Freeman (2003: 49) so eloquently puts it, 'the rules provide a modicum of security to language learners – they give them something to hold onto in the vast rush of noise that is the new language'.

Organising teaching materials, coursebooks and syllabuses around pedagogic grammar rules also simplifies matters and conforms to the expectations of many teachers and learners, especially those who strive for high levels of accuracy or those that need to pass an exam or test. Thornbury (1999) suggests that a focus on rules also gets teachers and learners straight to the point, and this is something that Swan (2006) says is vital when time is limited and learners have little exposure to the language outside the classroom. Many rules of form can be very simply and efficiently explained or deduced, and by taking this approach, learners often feel that they are learning something and making progress. This can be vital for their motivation.

A focus on rules and rule discovery also appeals to those adolescent and adult learners who enjoy the analytical nature of exploring forms, uncovering patterns and putting them to use in practice tasks. In fact, many students believe that knowing the rules will help them communicate and understand the language better. This may explain why of the many questions that L2 learners ask in class, a high proportion concern the application of rules. However, despite the fact that a focus on rules meets many learners' expectations about their courses and classes, teachers must take care not to take this focus to extremes and to avoid the situation where learners do not actually learn English, but grammar (Swan, 2002).

Of course, the security and comfort of our learners must be something that teachers should strive for, especially in view of the widely held belief that it is an important condition for successful language acquisition (eg. Krashen, 1982; Williams & Burden, 1997; Dörnyei, 2001). Nonetheless, the need to provide a kind of security blanket must not lead teachers to concentrate on grammar rules more than other equally important areas of language, such as collocations (*make a mistake, have a bad day*), fixed phrases (*as a matter of fact, by the way*) or formulaic frames or patterns (*the thing I like/love/hate most about it/him/them is …*). Equally, teachers with a good knowledge of grammar rules should not be tempted or encouraged to rely exclusively on more deductive teaching approaches at the expense of discovery learning, consciousness-raising, communicative practice or the development of receptive and productive skills. Though it may make the teacher feel comfortable, using a purely deductive approach goes against evidence that either supports a blend of deductive and inductive learning (eg. Haight *et al*, 2007; Ellis, 2008), or suggests that inductive learning is potentially more desirable (eg. Thornbury, 1997a; Brown, 2007).

The problem with rules

In much the same way that prescriptive grammarians believe rules to be fixed and unbreakable, many language teachers are taught to believe or come to accept that pedagogic grammar rules must be true, even when shown evidence to the contrary. One consequence of this is that for a lot of new and inexperienced teachers, their language awareness consists of what they have seen in coursebooks. It is not surprising that language learners end up with the same level of knowledge about language, therefore being confused when confronted with examples that do not conform to what they have been told by the expert or read in the textbook.

It is perhaps because they wish to prevent this type of confusion from happening in class that many teachers choose to work with decontextualised models of language and encourage learners to practise using new grammatical structures at sentence level. This is an approach to learning that many coursebooks continue to employ, despite the fact that it encourages learners to think more about the grammatical form of a language item and less about how it can be used for communicative purposes. The upshot of this is that learners are prevented from developing the skills or strategies needed to use the language to communicate specific meanings and messages (Nunan, 2003).

Sentence level practice can also mean that learners are forced into what Chalker (1994) calls 'arbitrary manipulations of form'. For example, learners may be asked to change active sentences into passive ones without really understanding why or when they would do so (Figure 1), or transforming direct speech into reported speech by back-shifting the main verb, for example, changing it from the present simple to the past simple (Figure 2).

This back-shifting is done despite the fact that 'She says she's sorry' and 'He says that he'll do it later' are equally valid in the examples.

Figure 1

> ### Rewrite the sentences in the passive, beginning with the highlighted words.
>
> Shakespeare wrote **Macbeth** in 1606.
>
> ➔ **Macbeth** *was written by Shakespeare in 1606.*
>
> 1. Jonathan Ive designed **the iPhone**.
> 2. Many Mediterranean and Middle Eastern countries produce **olive oil**.
> 3. *Johann Gottfried Galle* discovered **Neptune** in 1846.
> 4. Francis Ford Coppola directed **the *Godfather trilogy***.

Figure 2

> Listen to the following sentences in direct speech. Say them in reported speech. Begin in sentence with *He said …* or *She said …* and make sure you change the form of the main verb.
>
> 1. I'm sorry.'   ➔   She said that she was sorry
> 2. 'I'll do it later.'   ➔   He said that he would do it later

Exploring a foreign language in this way also means that learners will, more often than not, meet examples of language that are divorced from realistic contexts. This is problematic in itself, as 'decontextualised sentences which are "made up" for teaching purposes are nearly always over-simplified. The lexis is selected because we are sure that learners know it already and the structure of clauses and sentences is chosen to exemplify a specific teaching point without any other complications' (Willis, 2000). This ensures that the language seems neat and tidy, and creates a sense of comfort and security for the learners.

However, it is possible that relying on pedagogic grammar rules and practising the language at sentence level is in fact limiting how much progress the learners are able to make and potentially storing up trouble for later. As learners progress through the levels and meet the same forms in longer and more authentic stretches of language, they will come across what teachers and coursebooks have hidden from them or told them was not possible. For example, learners who have been taught that state verbs cannot be used in the progressive form might be surprised or confused when they come across perfectly acceptable examples such as these:

I'm loving every minute of it.
I'm not liking this. *I'm going.*
What *am I not understanding* about this?
Are you seriously *believing* all this?

As state verbs are here used in the progressive form, the basic rule, already embedded in their mind, will need to be modified by sub-rules and exceptions (Lewis, 2002) or in the very worst cases, discarded as inadequate. This is surely an issue worth avoiding in the first place.

A further issue with analysing language at sentence level rather than looking at it in texts is the fact that it enables teachers and materials writers to stick to broad generalisations about language, despite the fact that language operates at text rather than sentence level. Indeed, some areas of grammar, such as the tense system, modality and the use of articles, would be virtually impossible to learn simply through the study of model sentences and the application of rules alone. These areas of language would naturally be better understood and acquired if learners were to notice and explore them in texts (Willis, 2003). A case in point is this rule for the definite article:

■ The definite article is used when the listener or reader knows or can work out which particular person or thing we are talking about.

The reason that the listener or reader is able to identify the person or thing that is being referred to could be down to a number of factors: a) it has already been mentioned; b) the speaker explicitly says which one they mean; c) it is clear from the situation which one they mean. However, in a decontextualised sentence, it is quite hard for learners and teachers to know which of the above factors apply. A text, on the other hand, contains a lot more clues.

Consider this message I received from a friend:

Hi Danny

Sorry for <u>the short reply</u> before but <u>the guy</u> I'm running <u>the course</u> with at the moment is doing my head in. He's told <u>the trainees</u> that we'll put all <u>the materials</u> onto to this portal, so now I'm going to have to spend ages doing that.

In this email, none of the nouns with definite articles refer to things that have already been explicitly mentioned, so factor a) does not apply. Which factors do?

- When my friend writes 'Sorry for the short reply', he is referring to something we are both aware of but have not discussed, that is, a brief and slightly grumpy reply to an earlier invitation to meet up. It is therefore clear from the situation which reply my friend is referring to (factor c).

- When my friend then mentions 'the guy', he goes on to explain who he is writing about (factor b).

- Because my friend has now mentioned the course, it is subsequently clear which trainees and materials he is referring to in the last sentence (factor b).

However, another factor is at work in this email. My friend is able to use the definite article with such regularity because of our close relationship and the fact that we do very similar jobs. Therefore, when he mentions the course, the students and the materials, he knows that these things will generally be quite familiar to me and I will be able to work out what he means. So we have three reasons why my friend is able to use the definite article in this message, and these can only really be understood by exploring them within the text and by helping learners understand the relationship between the writer and the reader. It would be much harder to do this within decontextualised sentences.

Texts also provide important clues as to why certain tenses are used. Take for example the use of the past progressive below, which comes from a spoken anecdote.

So I would have been about eight or nine at the time, and we were staying at my grandmother's house in East Hoathly for the summer. So there was me, my brother and sister and my two cousins, and what we would do was go into this old sweet shop every day to stock up on sweets.

Here the past progressive is being used to set the scene or provide background information before the speaker moves on to the main events of the story. This is a very common usage of the tense, but one that is difficult to introduce at lower levels if it is explored at sentence level only. It is therefore preferable to help learners notice and practice this function by looking at and creating anecdotes and stories instead. An example of this can be seen in Lesson 7 on page 108.

Even when coursebook and materials writers do use texts as the stimuli for language study, some extremely common rules still need to be questioned. Take for example the use of the passive in this short extract from a news report:

> Two men from the North of England have been arrested after attempting to bring rare and protected animal species into the country via a London airport.

Generally, this kind of example sentence will be used in coursebooks to elicit or highlight this common rule:

■ We use the passive voice when the doer of the action is not known or not important.

However, there are a number of problems with this description. First, although it is designed to be simple, it is in fact quite vague, offering two possible reasons for the writer's use of the passive: 1) the doer is not known, or 2) the doer is not important. Clearly 1 is not correct as we know that some airport officials must have arrested the man. Therefore, it must be 2. Yet L2 learners often struggle with the idea of 'importance' as it is difficult to work out what it actually means. Why is the doer not important? After all, the doer (the people that arrested the men) clearly play an important role in the story and no doubt they would think this too. Perhaps the doer is 'not important' because it is obvious to the reader who it is, so there is no need for the writer to specify this. This, though, is not clear.

A further problem with the above description of the passive, and one common in many coursebooks, is the fact that the genre (news reports) is not given any attention. This means that learners are not informed that the passive is frequently used in news reports or that in this genre, rather than using the rule about the doer, it is more accurate to say that the passive is used to maintain topic focus and to structure information in such a way that enables the reader to start with understood or known information and to end with new (Eastwood, 2005).

Let us look at how this is done as the news report continues below.

> **Two men from the North of England <u>have been arrested</u>** after attempting to bring rare and protected animal species into the country via a London airport. *The men,* **aged 37 and 41, <u>were arrested</u> on Thursday (November 12) and have been released on bail pending further enquiries.**
>
> *Customs officers* **<u>were</u> first <u>alerted</u> to the men when they noticed what appeared to be holes <u>drilled</u> into the fabric of their cases.**
>
> **Bold:** new information
> *Italic:* known or understood information

In the article, the writer introduces new information in the first sentence (Two men from the North of England have been arrested). In the second sentence, the known or understood information then comes first (The men) and the new information (their ages, when they were arrested and the fact that they have been bailed) follows.

The pattern continues in the next paragraph, where the understood or known information (Customs officials) comes first, and the new information comes after (were first alerted). In this way, the journalist's writing follows a certain linear logic and the text is easier for the reader to follow.

However, because the passive is often explored and practised only at sentence level, and because coursebooks and grammars often only provide the vague and abstract rule about the doer, the actual reason that writers and speakers use the form has been hidden from both learners and language teachers. Thankfully, in some recent coursebooks, such as *English Unlimited* (Tilbury *et al*, 2011), this issue is being addressed.

The wording of the rules

Having seen earlier that language rules can be useful for some students, it is important to ensure that the rules we use are as effective as possible, and a key criteria is that a rule should always be true (eg. Swan, 1994; Ur, 2011). Although the use of simplified rules means that many coursebooks are not strictly sticking to this criteria, the way that they present rules suggests that they are. The same is true of a lot of teaching material. These 'broad-spectrum' rules, as Swan calls them, are often described using the present simple and the imperative form. There is also the tendency to use the pronouns *we* and *you*, as can be seen in these examples:

- The past progressive describes a longer past action interrupted by a shorter one.
- Use *going to* when a prediction is based on strong evidence
- We use *used to* to talk about past states, habits and routines that are no longer true.
- You use the passive when the speaker is not known or unimportant.

However, using the present simple or imperative along with the pronouns *we* and *you* suggests that the given rule is true for all users at all times, which as we have already seen, is not the case. In fact, the use of *we* and *you* implies there is no choice about using a particular form. Along with the vagueness of some grammatical descriptions, this casts doubt on the value of the rules themselves.

A final issue with the way that rules are presented is the use of adverbs of frequency in the descriptions. As Lewis (2002) states, 'Advice and classroom hints are one thing ... [but] rules cannot be given which include the words *sometimes* or *in certain circumstances*'. Clearly it is not a particularly useful rule if it is only true sometimes, but we do not know when. However, the rules presented to students in coursebooks and other teaching materials frequently include these words.

Let us look at an example. In the text below, in order to contextualise a number of examples of *used to* and *would* to describe past and present habits and routines, the writers use an interesting text about a woman who marries someone who seems to be addicted to online gaming. At the beginning of the text, she describes meeting her future husband.

> When I first met Sam I really liked him. He was kind and good looking, though quite shy. He <u>used to play</u> computer games – or one in particular – quite a lot. <u>I'd visit</u> him at this home and he'd be sitting at his computer. Sometimes he wouldn't even turn around.
>
> © Pearson education, 2011

However, the reader learns that after the couple got married and had a child Sam's gaming problem continued into the present day. In fact, the problem has become so extreme that by the end of the text, the writer is wondering whether she should leave her addicted husband. All in all the text is very interesting and has proved an engaging one for learners, often leading to lively discussions about what the writer should do and why she might have married the man in the first place (see Lesson 2 on page 90).

In a follow-up discovery activity, the learners are encouraged to use the text to uncover the following rule:

■ Use *used to* to talk about activities and states that happened regularly in the past but not usually now.

This is a common rule in coursebooks, and one that Parrott (2010) also proposes, describing *used to* and *would* as 'alternatives to the past simple in describing habits and repeated actions which took place over a period of time (and which often then ceased)'.

Although the two descriptions above are certainly true, and it is surely right that we acknowledge the fact that grammar is not a precise systematic framework, the use of *usually* or *often* can present a problem for learners who may want to know when they can use *used to* for describing a past habit or repeated action that has *not* ceased.

Perhaps the key here is to use texts such as the one above to explore 'the principle of general use' (Lewis, 2002) or what Larsen-Freeman (2003) terms as 'the reasons underlying the rules'. In Jade's story, the writer starts with a description of her future husband at the time that they met and introduces the fact that back then he played a lot of computer games. However, rather than saying that her husband eventually stopped playing computer games, she informs the reader that this habit continues to the present day. Perhaps it is because their circumstances have changed (they are now married with a child), or because she views their relationship differently, but in this instance Jade is able to use *used to* for describing a past habit that has not stopped.

It seems therefore that *used to* is *predominantly* used to describe past habits and routines that have stopped, and it is *occasionally* used to describe habits that still continue. However, it is *always* used to describe something that has changed between the past and the present, whether the action stops completely, is reduced or increased or, in some instances, continues under different circumstances. This can be seen in these examples:

He used to play computer games. (Before we got married.)
He used to play computer games. (Now he does not.)
He used to play computer games a lot more. (Now he plays less often.)
He used to play computer games a lot less. (Now he plays more often.)

Although this new description appears to be closer to the truth of the matter, it is important that we are sensitive to what our learners need. As Batstone (2007) suggests, we do not want to overload them with a list of subtle distinctions, yet nor do we want to provide them with simplifications that mean that they are unable to relate them to the examples they encounter outside the coursebook or to the meanings they wish to express. It would appear that a different solution is required.

Conclusion

To summarise, the major issues with the rules, other than the fact that some may be quite dubious, are that they are often somewhat vague or abstract, they are frequently separate from a context and text type, and they regularly ignore the decisions the writer or speaker makes when deciding what to say or write. By also using the present simple or the imperative, the pronouns *we* and *you*, and by frequently qualifying the rules with words like *often* and *usually*, the rules that teachers and learners end up relying on may not be particularly helpful. This is especially true once learners reach a stage when they begin to process more genuine stretches of language and start to encounter exceptions or variations. In short, the rules we use in class actually describe language *use* rather than how language is *used* by different writers or speakers at different times and for different purposes.

Along with the way that grammar is packaged and described for students as they begin the process of learning the language, a further issue lies in the use of the word 'rules' itself. 'Rules' naturally suggest a degree of regulation, creating the assumption that they cannot be broken. One solution lies in the way that we describe examples of language, perhaps not as rules but as 'idealisations' which learners can diverge from (Gnutzmann, 2005). Alternatively, teachers can view or describe the rules as 'useful hints', as Willis (2003) suggests, or 'rules of thumb' (Swan, 1994). Teachers could also be encouraged to explore 'principles of general use' (Lewis, 2002) or 'reasons' (Larsen-Freeman, 2003). Whatever term we use, descriptions of language can then be viewed as a helpful tool or template that learners can refer to as they begin the process of exploration that is learning a foreign language. If this is the case, learners will need to be encouraged to work with texts and samples of language so that they gradually question and refine their own understanding of the grammatical system and formulate their own descriptions.

Of course, during a lesson it is possible for a good teacher to provide their students with suitable descriptions of meaning, as they are able to match or adapt them to the circumstances, the learners' backgrounds, the materials they are using, the context of the lesson or, perhaps most importantly, to what the learners want to say or write. Here, it does not have to be a question of presenting students with a general rule, a hint or a principle. Instead, the teacher can lead learners towards a new understanding step by step, adjusting and rewording descriptions accordingly (Lewis, 2002). This, however, is arguably quite difficult for newer or less confident teachers to do, and as long as there is comfort and security to be found in the use of teaching materials and rules, it is understandable that many of us choose to continue to put our faith in them.

Without publishers making changes to the way that rules are described in their materials, and as long as new teachers are trained to work with these materials and with the rules as they are, the problems described above will continue. However, I believe that a creative solution can be found in the language classroom and in collaboration between teachers and their learners, and this will now be discussed in Chapter 3.

3. From rules to reasons

'When I use a word,' Humpty Dumpty said, *'it means just what I choose it to mean – neither more nor less.'*
Lewis Carroll

The previous chapters looked at different approaches to teaching grammar and explored the reasons why a focus on both meaning and form and the provision of meaningful language practice are essential parts of learning a second language in the classroom. They also explored the problem of relying solely on pedagogic grammar and coursebook rules, and it was suggested that teachers and learners should treat these rules with some degree of caution.

This chapter:

- introduces an alternative approach to analysing language in the L2 classroom

- looks at the reasons why analysing texts and exploring the communicative purpose of the writer or the speaker enables L2 learners to better understand and describe why a particular form is being used

- explains why learners' ability to do this means that language teachers have a credible alternative to the types of exercises and pedagogic grammar rules commonly found in coursebooks, grammars and language teaching materials.

However, before looking at the techniques and lesson procedures that teachers can use to help learners uncover reasons and create their own descriptions of meaning and usage, we will first discuss the difference between a rule and a reason.

The difference between rules and reasons

In her influential work, *Teaching Language: From grammar to grammaring*, Diana Larsen-Freeman (2003) makes a clear distinction between rules and reasons. First, rules tell us *how* we should use a certain form. They are designed to help teachers and students see what is correct and appropriate and what is not. Rules, therefore, help learners to understand what is possible and how to form accurate and appropriate sentences. Reasons, on the other hand, do not relate to accuracy. Instead, they tell us *why* we might use a certain form. They are far more flexible, and can be used to show teachers and learners how proficient speakers make choices about the language they use. They also show us why proficient language users are able to break the rules in order to say what they want to say.

To understand the difference between the two, let us look at the common pedagogic rule that tells us that state verbs cannot be used in progressive forms, which we saw in Chapter 2. As *own* is a state verb, the following example would not be possible:

He is owning a really expensive car. †

However, Larsen-Freeman claims that it is not only the rule that makes this example incorrect or inappropriate. It is also due to the fact that in English, the speaker would most likely view owning an expensive car as an unchanging state. In other words, they see ownership as something fixed. At the time of speaking he owns the car, and if he were to sell it, he would simply no longer own it. This is the way it is, and because the speaker sees this situation as permanent, he does not use a progressive form. This is the reason behind the rule.

The same reason can be seen at work in the following example of the state verb *love*. This time it is 'used correctly' with a simple, not progressive verb form:

I love my job.

Here, the speaker views their feelings about their job as permanent and unchanging in much the same way as the previous speaker viewed owning his car. Of course, new management may come in and implement unpopular changes. In which case, the speaker would no longer love their job, or at least they might begin to feel less positive about it. However, at the time of speaking, the way they feel is fixed and unchanging. For this reason, rather than because of the rule, the progressive form would not be used.

The idea that there is a reason behind the rule can be seen more simply in the following diagram.

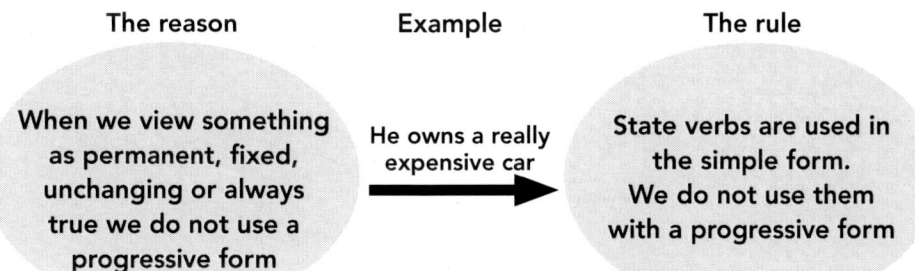

However, what happens if the speaker does not have fixed and unchanging feelings about their job? What happens if they wish instead to describe the fact that their feelings are intensifying, shifting or are somehow different to the way they usually are? In this case, the speaker might choose to say:

I love my job at the moment.
or
I'm loving my job.

In the first sentence, the speaker has followed the rule relating to state verbs and used a simple form. This means that he or she has to use a time expression to show that their feelings are unusual or different in some way. Without a time expression, the situation sounds permanent. However, in the second sentence the rule relating to state verbs and progressive forms has been broken. But how is this possible? It is because rather than viewing their feelings as a permanent state, the speaker is instead describing a change or fluctuation in the way they feel. This is not how they normally view their job, and this new perspective may in fact be quite surprising. For this reason, the usual rule given about state verbs and the use of the progressive no longer applies. Because the speaker's feelings about their job are different from the norm, the progressive form may in this case be used. In short, the reason overrides or bypasses the rule. This can be seen in the following diagram.

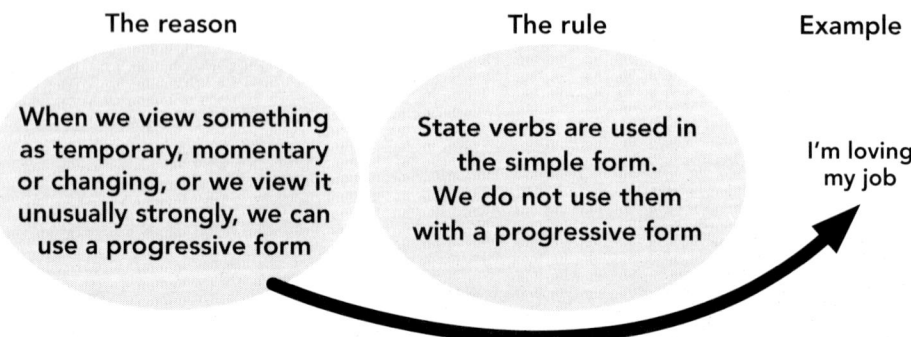

The reason	The rule	Example
When we view something as temporary, momentary or changing, or we view it unusually strongly, we can use a progressive form	State verbs are used in the simple form. We do not use them with a progressive form	I'm loving my job

Notice the use of the modal verb *can* in the description of the reason. This demonstrates how flexible our choice of grammar actually is. It also shows how grammar allows us to make new meanings, express subtle differences, create nuances and indicate our perception of events and situations. Rules, on the other hand, are far more static, and it is this difference between rules and reasons that helps to explain why some of the issues we explored in the previous chapter exist in the first place.

It is therefore important that teachers seek to understand the reasons behind the rules. With this knowledge, it is easier to appreciate why users of English use the grammar they do and how speakers and writers are able to bypass the rules so frequently. In the process, it becomes clear that meaning is not somehow secondary to form, and that speakers of English do not have to strictly follow the rules in order to communicate effectively. Reasons allow teachers to see why things are the way they are, which helps them better understand the apparent arbitrariness of some grammar explanations (Larsen-Freeman, 2015). This in turn can provide a level of security that a vague or abstract rule cannot.

The importance of the speaker or writer

For language students, however, there is a much simpler way of exploring and understanding reasons. Instead of viewing reasons as the explanation for grammar rules, as we have seen above, it is easier to look at them as the explanation for the moment by moment choices that speakers or writers make when communicating their message. For students to understand this concept better, we need to go beyond single sentences and look at longer stretches of language. In other words, we need to look at examples of language use in texts. Take the following example. In this letter, the writer is telling a friend or close acquaintance about their job.

> I know I normally go on about how much I hate working at xxxxx but <u>I'm loving</u> it there at the moment. I don't think they've changed that much and xxxxx is still there but it just feels like <u>we're all pulling</u> in the same direction for a change and <u>no-one's trying</u> to take all the glory. It's like it's a totally different place.

Once again, we see the state verb *love* used in the progressive form. However, by looking at the example in a text such as this, we can discover why the writer or speaker chooses to do this. To help us understand the reason, we can ask ourselves the following question:

Why is the writer using a progressive form?

The reason is simple. It is because he does not normally feel this way about his job. At the beginning of the text, the writer makes it clear that he does not usually enjoy his work. At this particular moment in time, however, things are different. Everyone is pulling in the same direction (they don't normally) and no-one is trying to take all the credit (someone usually tries to). At this particular time therefore, the writer is loving his job.

By looking at language in this way, we can again understand how the speaker or writer is able to bypass the rule, as can be seen in the following diagram.

Example	The rule	The reason

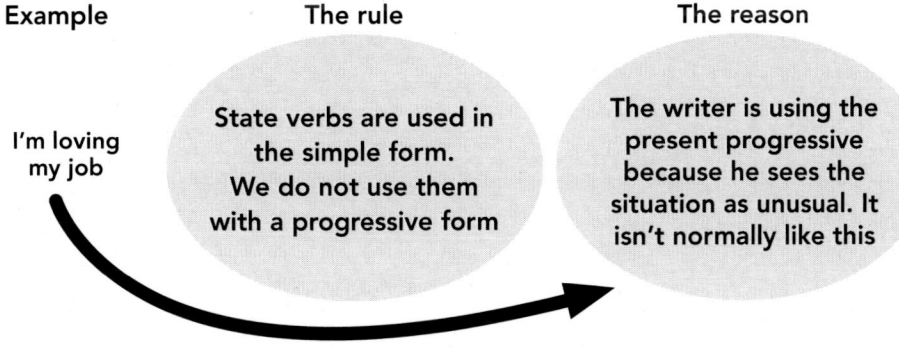

I'm loving my job

State verbs are used in the simple form. We do not use them with a progressive form

The writer is using the present progressive because he sees the situation as unusual. It isn't normally like this

Note that in the diagram above, the example from the text comes first. This is due to the fact that we are analysing the reason that lies behind the writer's choice of language, as opposed to analysing language use in general. It is also important to note that while the present simple is used in the rule (*We do not use*), a progressive form (*is using*) is used to describe the reason. This is significant, as using the progressive rather than the present simple enables us to demonstrate that the use of the form depends on the speaker's intentions at *this particular moment*. It is not a fixed idea but something that is entirely context dependent.

Where the present simple creates the impression that rules are static and fixed, a progressive form helps us see reasons as dynamic, non-permanent or ongoing within the current situation (Yule, 1998). There is also the potential for change, as we can allow for the fact that what may be appropriate in one instance may not be so in next. The progressive also enables us to view the action from the inside. It is the writer who is making the choice, and their decision is based on what they want to communicate at the moment of writing or speaking. This is why the rule need not apply.

A standard text-based procedure

So how can L2 learners be encouraged to uncover reasons? Happily, it is not necessary for a teacher to make radical changes to the way they might structure a lesson. Instead, the technique can be embedded within two standard lesson procedures. The first is a text-based approach, in which learners begin by processing a written or spoken text for meaning before they analyse it for form. The second approach involves the use of tasks.

Let us start with the text-based language lesson, an example of which is outlined on page 53. Here, the lesson is broken up into stages, but for a complete version, see page 187. In a standard text-based language lesson, the teacher begins by engaging students in the topic of the lesson and providing a motivation for reading or listening (Pre-readings 1 & 2).

The Passive

Pre-reading 1: Work in pairs and discuss the following questions.

- What items are illegal to bring into your country?
- Why are these items illegal?
- What is the punishment for bringing these items into the country?

Pre-reading 2: Read the headline below. Work in pairs. What do you think the police discovered in the luggage?

> Police make wild discovery in airport luggage

The learners then read or listen to the text in order to get an idea of the general meaning. This is most commonly done through the use of gist tasks, in which learners read the text quickly to establish the main idea (Reading 1) and/or comprehension questions (Reading 2).

Reading 1:

Police make wild discovery in airport luggage

A 50-year-old Londoner <u>has been arrested</u> at a UK airport for attempting to bring body parts, bones and eggs from a range of protected species into the country in his luggage. After <u>being stopped and questioned</u> by airport police and customs officials, commercial premises belonging to the man's family <u>were searched</u> and various illegal items <u>were seized</u> and <u>taken away</u> for testing. Amongst a large haul of uncertified items, police found turtle shells and eggs as well as bottles of snake wine, a drink <u>believed</u> to have restorative and curative powers in many parts of Asia.

The smuggled wildlife <u>were listed</u> as endangered by CITES (Convention on International Trade in Endangered Species), and the seized animals <u>will be handed over</u> to the Department of the Environment to establish if they <u>can be returned</u> to their country of origin.

The accused, who claimed the animals were for private collections and gifts, <u>has been released</u> on bail pending further enquiries.

Reading 2: Read the article again and answer the following questions.
1. Where is the man from?
2. Where was he arrested?
3. What species of animals were found in his luggage?
4. What will happen to the animals?
5. What reason did the man give for smuggling the animals?

Once general meaning has been established, the learners are given questions or provided with prompts that enable them to discover or formulate a predetermined grammar rule or a set of rules (Grammar 3a & 3b). When the teacher is confident that the learners have understood these rules, they are given the opportunity to practise using the new language. This might be done either through the use of controlled practice activities (Exercise 1), in which the students work on manipulating the form and developing accuracy, or through a freer practice task. This would involve more extensive or genuine opportunities for students to use the new language for communicative purposes. The lesson then finishes with feedback, in which the students' use of the new language is explored.

Grammar 3a: Look at the sentences from the text. Then answer questions 1–4.

   a. *A 50-year-old Londoner has been arrested.*
   b. *Police have arrested a 50-year-old Londoner.*
   1. What is the subject of each sentence?
   2. In which sentence is the focus on the smuggler? What kind of sentence is this?
   3. In which sentence is the focus on the police? What kind of sentence is this?
   4. In which sentence can we use *by* to say who does the action (the agent)?

Grammar 3b: Look at the sentences. Then choose the correct phrase to complete the rule.

   a. *A 50-year-old Londoner <u>has been arrested</u> for attempting to bring rare and protected species into the country.*
   ■ We use the passive when the doer (the agent) is *known/not known* or *important/not important*.

Exercise 1: Put the verbs in the brackets into the correct form, using the passive or the active.

1. More than 10,000 people _____ (arrest) at UK airports every year.
2. Police _____ (interview) the man for four hours.
3. The man's homes _____ (search) but no further evidence _____ (find).
4. The man _____ (claim) that they had bought the animals at a well-known tourist market.
5. The man _____ (release) on bail pending further enquiries.
6. Many endangered animals _____ (sell) for their medicinal properties.

The lesson procedure is summarised as follows.

1. The teacher engages students in the topic of the lesson or text. This stage generates interest in the text, gives the learners a reason to process the text for meaning and activates learners' schemata (their background knowledge of the topic).
2. The learners process the text for meaning by answering gist and/or comprehension questions. If learners do not have a basic understanding of the text the discovery learning that follows this stage will be very difficult.
3. The learners are encouraged to notice an aspect of language and discover patterns, meanings and rules. This can be accompanied by a teacher-led presentation stage.
4. The learners are given the opportunity to use the new language in controlled and perhaps freer practice activities.
5. Learners receive feedback on their use of the new language.

Uncovering reasons in texts

However, in order to help our learners uncover reasons instead of rules, the teacher needs to make some subtle yet important adjustments to this standard procedure.

First, as well as processing the text for the general meaning (point 2 in the lesson procedure above), the learners must also identify the genre, the writer and the reader. They also need to identify the purpose of the text. Do this yourself before you continue reading.

Police make wild discovery in airport luggage

A 50-year-old Londoner <u>has been arrested</u> at a UK airport for attempting to bring body parts, bones and eggs from a range of protected species into the country in his luggage. After <u>being stopped and questioned</u> by airport police and customs officials, commercial premises belonging to the man's family <u>were searched</u> and various illegal items <u>were seized</u> and <u>taken away</u> for testing. Amongst a large haul of uncertified items, police found turtle shells and eggs as well as bottles of snake wine, a drink <u>believed</u> to have restorative and curative powers in many parts of Asia.

The smuggled wildlife <u>were listed</u> as endangered by CITES (Convention on International Trade in Endangered Species), and the seized animals <u>will be handed over</u> to the Department of the Environment to establish if they <u>can be returned</u> to their country of origin.

The accused, who claimed the animals were for private collections and gifts, <u>has been released</u> on bail pending further enquiries.

The text is of course an article from a newspaper, although it has been adapted for teaching purposes. The writer is therefore a journalist. The purpose of the text is primarily to report the news, while the play on words in the headline is designed to attract the readers' attention.

This additional stage of identifying the genre and the purpose of the text not only helps students develop a better understanding of the intended meanings being communicated. It also means that in the discovery stage that follows the learners are better able to 'look beyond the formal rules operating within sentences, and consider the people who use the language and the world in which it happens' (Cook, 1989). In other words, it helps students understand how the text type, the participants and the context all play a part in determining the choice of language used.

Wherever possible, it is also important to encourage the learners to read the text in the same way that they would in real life. Therefore, rather than use traditional comprehension questions, as seen in the lesson material (Reading 2 on page 54), it is better to ask questions that elicit feelings or opinions. For example, two effective questions for this text would be 'How does this article make you feel?' or 'What punishment should the man receive?' Questions such as these ensure that rather than merely demonstrating that they understand a set of specific facts from the text, the learners are encouraged to engage with the content far more. This not only provides a deeper level of understanding but also primes the learners for the discovery work that follows.

The second adjustment to the standard procedure relates to the way that the meanings and uses of specific language items are articulated or presented, and it is here that we move away from rules and start to look at reasons. As we saw earlier, the text about the smuggler is designed to introduce or review the passive, and in the model lesson (Grammar 3b on page 54), the learners are guided towards the following rule:

We use the passive when the doer (the agent) is not known or not important.

However, as we have already seen, there are a number of problems with this rule:

- The genre, the writer and the purpose of the text are not taken into consideration.

- The materials writer uses the present simple to convey the rule. They also use the pronoun *we*. For many teachers and L2 learners, this wording suggests that the rule is true for all users at all times, which as we have seen in Chapter 2, is clearly not the case.

- The learners are given two possible reasons why the writer might have used the passive, which can make the rule seem vague and ambiguous.

- Learners often struggle with the idea of the word 'importance'.

In addition to problems with the rule, the guided discovery activity (Grammar 3b) also lacks challenge. First, it is highly possible that learners at B1 level will have already encountered this rule in a grammar book or a previous lesson. This may mean that students end up articulating a rule that they have seen before rather than truly learning something new about the language. In addition, when it comes to discovering the meaning and determining why the writer uses the passive, the learners are only given one possible usage. This means that every student in the class is prompted to 'discover' the same thing, thereby giving learners little room to make their own interpretations or come to their own conclusions. Therefore, if learners are only given limited options that lead them towards generic rules of thumb, it is possible that coursebook discovery activities are not actually doing what they set out to do.

To uncover reasons, it is necessary to go beyond the rule and to increase the chance of the learners discovering something new. To do this, we have to change how we elicit understanding of language items and the way that learners formulate descriptions. This can be done with the following prompts:

Why is the writer using the passive in this text?
Why is the journalist using the passive in this article?
The writer is using the passive to/because ...
The journalist is using the passive to/because ...

These frames and question forms offer an immediate solution to the problems outlined above. First, both the teacher and the learners are encouraged to focus on the role of the writer. This in turn adds a greater level of focus on the genre, which helps learners better understand the fact that different text types have distinctive styles and characteristics and that the choice of language is down to the writer or the speaker. The use of the present progressive (*The writer is using ...*) in the prompts reinforces this. It also means that rather than looking at potential meanings and choices, only one meaning need be explored – the one that the writer intends to convey at this particular moment.

The use of the present progressive rather than the present simple also means that instead of mechanically quoting a half-digested rule, learners are more likely to come up with descriptions of how the language is being used by the writer or speaker. This can greatly add to learners' security and confidence, as it allows them to see why things are the way they are, thus 'reducing the arbitrariness of grammar explanations' (Larsen-Freeman, 2015).

The learners are also encouraged to describe the meaning in their own words so that vague or misleading terms like 'important' can be avoided. We have also taken away the need for students to rely on their understanding of metalanguage or grammatical terminology. To make things simpler still, students can even formulate the reason in their L1 if they wish.

Yet are L2 learners really capable of creating and articulating their own reasons? The simple answer is yes, though it is necessary to stress that they need time and guidance in order to do so, as they would when developing any new skill. However, the examples below, taken from adult students at B1 and B2 level, clearly show that learners do have the potential to understand and articulate reasons. In fact, it is not uncommon to see them go beyond the rule in the book and discover something new, as these students have in noticing how the passive is used by journalists to maintain topic focus and to introduce new information.

> Because first he introduce the man then he wants to keep focus on the man.†
>
> Because first we know the man and it happens to the man. Then we can know the others and it happens to the others.†
>
> First he talks about the smuggler. Then he is using the passive so you see it's still about the smuggler.

Once the learners have articulated their reasons and explored their descriptions with the class and the teacher, they are now ready to move on to practice. This is where we find the third major adjustment to the procedure.

The use of replication tasks

In a standard text-based lesson, discovery activities are often followed by controlled practice exercises such as gap-fills or sentence completion activities. However, where these types of exercise are designed to help students develop accuracy and manipulate the form of a specific language item, they do not enable learners to start using the language for communicative purposes. Because controlled practice is also often done at sentence level, and because there is usually only one correct answer, it also means that the practice can be quite mechanical. This can lead to the all too common situation of learners knowing the rule and being able to provide an example sentence, such as 'the ice cream was eaten by the boy', yet they are not capable of using the structure in genuine, communicative ways.

In order to prevent this from happening, and to help learners better understand and assimilate the reasons they have discovered, practice tasks should instead enable students to use structures for genuine communicative purposes. So rather than doing controlled practice exercises, the students should instead create their own texts. In order to maximise the chance that the learners use the new language, the best activities to use are *replication* and *transposition* tasks.

What are replication tasks? These are meaningful, creative and open-ended communicative activities in which learners recreate or reconstruct texts that are similar to the one they have analysed for meaning. In the model lesson about the smuggler, therefore, the students might summarise the text to a partner, reconstruct it from memory or write their own newspaper article from a different headline, such as the one below.

Because replication tasks recreate the same text type that the students have analysed for meaning, they naturally enable learners to use the target language for the same purpose as the writer or the speaker. This means that during the practice, the learners are able to think about usage as well as form and accuracy. This is an important part of a learner's development, because when language input is disassociated from usage it is more difficult for learners to understand what they are learning and what to do with it (Larsen-Freeman, 2015). It also means that teachers are often unable to assess whether their learners are able to use the target structure for communicative purposes. The focus instead is on how accurately they form it.

Replication tasks, however, enable learners to focus on both meaning and form. This can be seen in the following example of student work, in which a language learner at B2 level has reconstructed the text found in the model lesson.

A 50 years old man has been arrested at Gatwick airport for smuggling body parts of animals into the UK in his luggage. After the police stopped him and questioned him about the items, his shop was searched and illegal items was founded and seized

On the whole, the learner is having little trouble forming the passive, producing it correctly in both the present perfect (*has been arrested*) and the past simple (*was searched*). He is, however, displaying a problem with verb-noun agreement (*items was*) and the form of the irregular verb *find* (*founded*). This is something that can briefly be explored in feedback.

The student has also been very successful in terms of creating a meaningful and coherent introduction to the article, using both the active and the passive to do so. However, the journalist has maintained topic focus more effectively. This was done by using the passive in the second sentence (*After being stopped and questioned by airport police …*) in order to keep the focus on the smuggler. The student, on the other hand, changes the subject and switches to the active, so focusing more on the police (*After the police stopped him and questioned him …*). Although this is clear and accurate, the teacher can use this example from the replication task in a feedback stage to provide the learner with further input into how the passive is used to maintain topic focus.

While still providing a focus on form, replication tasks can also be freer and offer the learners more opportunities to be creative. This can be seen in the following example, in which two learners have written their own article using only a new headline as a prompt.

WOMAN ARRESTED OVER NINETEEN-YEAR OVERDUE RENTAL VIDEO

When Blockbuster closed its last store in Putney discovered that one of its clients hadn't gave back one of its VHS tapes for 19 years.

The due amont exceeded the maximum punishable as a misdemeanor, so a complaint was filed as a felony.

The police arrived to the accused's house holding a search warrant, the house was searched, the tape was found and the womas was arrested.

After being presented to the judge, the woman stated that she had completely forgotten that she had the tape, but the police report showed that it had be used to record private scenes. For that reason, a private property offence was added to the sentence.

The woman was sentenced to pay £7000 fine and a year of community works.

As with the earlier text reconstruction task, this freer piece of writing enables the teacher to explore both the students' use of the passive and how well they can form it. Because the task is free, there is also the potential to explore a range of lexical items, for example, the collocations *ordered to pay* and *given community service* as opposed to *sentenced to life* or *sentenced to five years*. Perhaps if the teacher is feeling brave, they might also wish to explore the phrase *used to record private scenes!*

Replication tasks also enable learners to integrate the target language with other known language, which is harder to achieve in sentence level controlled practice exercises. This means that if the students are not actually having problems using the language item that they have been exploring, there is still the potential for the teacher to work with other issues that emerge. In the text about the overdue video, for example, where the learners are having little trouble forming the passive, they are having less success with perfect forms (*hadn't gave back †/ had be used †*). This would be a useful issue to address.

Because replication tasks provide different challenges for students, they are very suitable for classes with mixed abilities. For example, where a more confident student might choose to do the task as a free writing activity, another may prefer to take their time and plan what they want to say. Alternatively, another learner might prefer to complete the activity by writing individual sentences. These examples of self-differentiation mean that the learners are able to work with different levels of challenge, and the teacher is able to help learners at the level they have set themselves.

The following are examples of replication tasks. Note that because these tasks provide different levels of challenge, a teacher can offer their learners a choice as to which one they would like to do:

- Students reconstruct a short text from memory.

- Students reconstruct a text using key words or content words as prompts.

- Students reconstruct a text or part of a text after listening to a text and taking notes. This activity is often known as a 'dictogloss'.

- Students complete a text. For example, they create an ending or alternative ending to a story, anecdote or news report. They can also write another verse of a song or poem.

- Students recreate a text from the perspective of a different participant. For example, after reading or listening to a story, the students tell the story from the viewpoint of another character or bystander.

- Students create a text in the same medium. For example, after reading a restaurant review or a recipe, the learners write their own.

- Students personalise the activity. For example, after listening to an anecdote or childhood memory, the learners tell their own story or anecdote.

The use of transposition tasks

How is a transposition task different? Again, these are communicative tasks, but rather than producing or reconstructing a text so that it mirrors the structure and style of the original, in a transposed text the content is organised or recreated in a different medium or style. For example, the students can use their imaginations to turn the contents of the newspaper article about the smuggler into a police interview. This would entail half the class playing the role of the police and half the class pretending to be smugglers. Once the police have prepared questions and the smugglers have prepared their stories, the smugglers are interrogated. Alternatively, the text could be rewritten as a police report or letter from the smuggler to his parents or partner.

The term 'transposition' was coined by Gérard Genette (1997), a French literary theorist, and famous examples of transposition exist in many fields of the arts. For example, James Joyce's *Ulysses* transposed the events from Homer's *Odyssey* to modern day Dublin. In the world of film, Kurosawa's *Seven Samurai* was recreated as a Western in *The Magnificent Seven*, and in the theatre, Sondheim reworked *Romeo and Juliet* into the musical *WestSide Story*.

It is important to note here that where a replication task naturally provides learners with an opportunity to use the target language, a transposition task might not necessarily do so. This is due to the fact that a replication task involves the learners recreating a specific text type, so they use the target language in the same way as the original writer or speaker. However, if students role-play journalists interviewing the police, there may be no actual need for either to use the passive. This means that the teacher can compare how the passive might be used in one text type (a news report) but not in another (an interview). This subsequently provides the opportunity to raise awareness of the fact that different genres might use different forms to communicate the same message or events.

The following are examples of transposition tasks. Again, because these tasks provide different levels of challenge, the learners can choose the one they would like to do:

- Students turn a written article in a newspaper into a spoken report. This might even involve the use of reporters in the studio and the field.

- Students turn the contents of a song into a letter or a news report.

- Students turn an extract from a novel or graded reader into a film script or a radio play.

- Students turn a magazine article or diary entry into an interview.

- Students turn the contents of part of a biography into a chat show.

- Students take an extract from a guidebook and turn it into a leaflet, poster or presentation.

- Students turn a poem into a short story or a speech.

- Students turn a formal letter into an informal email or text message.

- Students turn the events in a short story into a fairy tale.

Why use replication and transposition tasks?

Along with the fact that replication and transposition tasks are engaging, fun and encourage the students to be creative, there are other important reasons for incorporating these types of tasks into our teaching. First, it is more likely that the grammar we teach and help learners to discover will take hold if there are frequent opportunities for learners to put it to practical use. Of course learners can still do controlled practice exercises or form-focused activities, but putting language to use should involve students using language creatively in interaction (Thornbury, 2004). Replication and transposition tasks do this.

Replication and transposition tasks are controlled in some senses, especially in the way that they provide opportunities for repetition. However, there is a key difference between repetition in these types of task and the kind found in controlled practice exercises. In a communicative task, the language that students use is more meaningful and relevant in that they have to create the ideas and the message themselves. Communicative tasks also encourage learners to relate form to meaning by showing how grammatical structures are used in real-life situations. Practice is therefore more authentic and not merely a mechanical parroting of sentence level structures (Swain & Lapkin, 2008).

Replication and transposition tasks are also slightly controlled in the sense that there is a degree of planning involved. This makes them extremely useful, as Nation (1996) suggests that there are some items of language that might only be available to learners in planned use rather than freer communicative tasks. Included in this might be a language item such as relative clauses. Replication activities such as text reconstruction or text extensions are a solution to this problem, as rather than transforming sentences or gap-filling texts, the learners can be encouraged to incorporate relative clauses into meaningful stretches of language.

The feedback loop

In output stages, there will be occasions when learners become aware of problems they are having with the language, and noticing these issues can subsequently help students to modify what they are trying to say or write (Swain & Lapkin, 1995). However, the teacher also needs to monitor student-to-student communicative stages, as there will be frequent instances when learners are unaware of the problems they are having. This is especially true if the errors students are making do not impede communication or prevent them from completing a task. Therefore, it is important that teachers are prepared to intervene during communicative stages to help learners identify gaps or to input language that would enable them to complete the task more effectively. Teachers can also monitor more unobtrusively so that they have space and time to note down language that can be explored in post-task feedback sessions.

In order to maximise the effectiveness of post-task feedback and to encourage learners to reflect on the language they have used, the teacher can use a feedback loop. In a feedback loop, the teacher uses the reasons that learners identified in the discovery stage to help them modify their output or assess how effectively they are using a certain form. This can be seen in the following exchange, in which the teacher intervenes as two students, playing the role of politicians, prepare their pledges before role-playing a classroom election.

Earlier in the lesson, the class had listened to two texts. The first text was a recording of two teachers discussing what they would do if they were in charge of running the country. The second was a video of a politician making promises in a victory pledge. After discussing the different roles of the speakers and identifying the purpose of each recording, the students then focused on the differences between *would* (used by the two teachers) and *will* (used by the politician). The group subsequently agreed on the following pair of reasons:

1. The politician is using *will* because he has the power. It's like a promise.
2. The two teachers are using *would* because they don't have the power.

However, while making notes and preparing to make their pledges, the two students have chosen to use *would* rather than *will*, writing 'We would make a cinema in the school so students can watch English films and pay less money'. Note how the teacher draws their attention to this and helps them modify what they want to say:

Teacher:	Have a look at this one. (Points to example of *would*.)
Student 2:	This one?
Teacher:	Yeah. Is <u>would</u> good here?
Student 1:	(pause) It's not good?
Teacher:	Mm … well you don't sound very sure.
	(pause)
Teacher:	How did the man on the video do it?
Student 1:	(pause, looking at the tape-script) He says *will*.
Teacher:	Right, <u>what's the reason?</u>

Continued

	(pause)
Student 1:	He …
Teacher:	… Here (pointing to student notes). Sorry go on.
Student 1:	He's got the power.
Student 2:	It's like a promise.
Teacher:	Yeah, and what are you doing now?
Student 1:	Making a promise.
Teacher:	Why?
Student 1:	To win.
Teacher:	You want to win, right. And do you have the power?
Student 2:	If we win.
Teacher:	Yeah. So *will* sounds better here.

The 'video' is a YouTube clip of Tony Abbot, the former prime minister of Australia, making election pledges in a victory speech.

As you can see, the teacher was able to use the reasons that the class had formulated earlier to help the two students modify what they wanted to say in their pledges. He was also able to exploit the tapescript and the speaker's communicative purpose to help make the concept clearer. Note there was no need for the teacher to use any complex terminology or abstract ideas. He was simply able to point to the fact that the speaker in the recording has power and wants to win the election. This is the reason the learners had formulated earlier in the lesson, and bringing it into play helped the two students upgrade what they wanted to say.

Monitoring and correcting students in this way does more than help them perform speaking tasks more effectively. It also encourages them to notice gaps in their language use or their understanding of a particular form. This in turn reinforces the input that came earlier. In fact, as it is possible that correction is more likely to be effective at the moment when the learner knows what they want to say and is trying to say it (Lightbown, 1992), there is a strong rationale for assisting students in this way.

However, it is also useful to explore learner language in post-discussion feedback stages. This is something that teachers often do, especially if they prefer not to intervene during genuine student-to-student interactions. Instead, the teacher monitors and notes down errors or examples of interesting or useful language. When the learners have finished speaking, the teacher writes these examples on the board or on a handout for follow-up language work. Typically, this will involve the students identifying the error or inappropriate form and attempting to correct or reformulate it. Once the learners are ready, the teacher then elicits the corrections or reformulations and records them on the board.

> **We ~~would~~ change the start of school from 09.00 to 09.30**
> Will

It is of course unclear why a learner might have made this error during the communicative activity. It could be because they have misunderstood or only partially understood the difference between *will* and *would*, or it might just have been a slip of the tongue. The issue may not necessarily even be a linguistic one. It might have been caused by the fact that the student did not yet see themselves in the role of a politician. If this is the case, *would* for a hypothetical situation is actually the more natural choice. However, a delayed correction slot gives the teacher the opportunity to provide further clarification of the target language, and to help with this, the teacher can again refer back to the reasons that the learners formulated earlier in the lesson. This is important, as though there is a delay between the moment of the error and the correction, there is still a focus on the communicative function of the language item. In this case, it is the way that *will* is used to make pledges and promises.

A delayed correction slot with a focus on reasons also helps the students reflect on what they have learnt during the lesson. Indeed, it is a good idea to round off the class with a brief moment of reflection, and this can be done by asking any of the following questions:

Why were we using *will* and *would* today?
Why were we using *would* when we talked about new laws for London?
But why did we use *will* when we made our pledges?

For learners, correction and reflection stages such as these can become part of a wider process of recognising errors and noticing gaps in their understanding, or of reflecting on success, progress and important realisations. In addition, reflection stages can help the teacher underline the value of exploring reasons and reiterate how they influence the choices that speakers of English make at different times and in different contexts.

A task-based approach

We have seen how a standard text-based procedure can be adapted to encourage learners to explore reasons rather than rules and how students then consolidate this learning by doing replication or transposition tasks. However, it is also possible to help learners uncover reasons without using texts, and this can be done by using Task-based Learning (TBL) as an approach.

In TBL, the starting point of the lesson is a communicative task in which the learners achieve a specific outcome (Willis, 1996). For example, they might choose the most appropriate candidate for a job, plan a class trip or describe how to cook their favourite recipes. The primary focus of these tasks is meaning, and the learners are free to use whatever language they want in order to successfully communicate their message.

The level of guidance given to the learners in a task-based lesson can vary hugely. One option is to give learners no guidance at all, either in terms of language assistance or preparation time. Instead, they go straight into the task. Although this is possibly a daunting prospect, it does have the benefit of giving the learners practice at coping with real-time interaction and genuine communicative situations (Willis & Willis, 2007). If there is a focus on form in this lesson, it does not then take place until after the students complete the task. However, a language focus might be required at moments when linguistic problems are encountered (Larsen-Freeman, 2001). This procedure can be described as a 'deep-end communicative approach', as there is no explicit focus or insistence on a set language item. Instead, the learners use whatever language they have available to complete the task. In this type of approach to learning, it is presumed that the learners acquire the language unconsciously by doing the task (Thornbury, 1999) or by noticing features of the language in any feedback or correction stage that follows.

The tasks that students perform in this deep-end version of TBL can therefore be seen as 'unfocused tasks'. These are tasks designed purely for communicative purposes rather than the practice of a specific linguistic feature (Ellis, 2003). This means that learners are able to call on whatever language they can in order to successfully complete the task. As we have seen above, however, using unfocused tasks and a deep-end approach to TBL does not necessarily mean that there is no language input. It just means that what the teacher focuses on is a lot less predictable.

Alternatively, teachers can choose to offer far more guidance, and this can be done in a number of ways. For example, students could be given preparation time in which they can think about what they want to say, look up words in a dictionary, make notes or confer with a partner. During this stage, the level of support that the tutor provides can also vary. On one hand, they can monitor and offer advice, feed in useful expressions or ideas, or even provide handouts containing language that the learners might use in their tasks. On the other hand, the teacher can be available to offer help, but only if the students ask for it. An example of a more guided task-based procedure can be seen here.

Battersea Power Station

Objective: students decide on an alternative use for Battersea Power station (or an iconic building in another city). They then present their ideas to the class.

1. The teacher starts the lesson by displaying pictures of Battersea Power station in South London. The students discuss the pictures and say what they know about it.
2. The teacher tells the students that the building is going to be turned into luxury flats and that many Londoners are disappointed by what is happening to such an iconic building.
3. The students are put into pairs. They have to think of five alternative uses for the building. The only criterion is that it must remain open to the public. Both students need to note down their ideas.
4. Once each pair has thought of at least three potential uses for the building, they are put into small groups or new pairings. The new groups must now choose which of their ideas they will present to the class.
5. Pre-task: once the students have chosen, they spend time preparing to tell the rest of the class what they propose to do with the power station and why it will benefit Londoners. The teacher monitors and helps the learners with language and ideas.

Continued

6. When they are ready, each group presents their idea to the class.
7. The students vote for the best proposal.
8. The teacher conducts a feedback session focusing on task achievement and learners' use of language.

It is worth noticing here that many teachers use texts or recordings as models to help learners prepare for tasks, as these can give the students a better sense of the structure of the genre or provide input on the kind of language needed to perform the task. However, as we have already looked at the way that texts can be used to help learners explore reasons, this will not be covered in the next section.

Exploring reasons in task-based lessons

In a guided task-based lesson, there are two main stages in which it is possible to focus on language and explore reasons. The first opportunity comes in the pre-task stage. In this part of the lesson, the teacher can either provide the learners with useful language models, or they can work with the language that the learners are planning to use. Either way, the teacher can use the same techniques of the feedback loop described earlier in this chapter. The difference here is that as language patterns have not yet been focused on, the learners have not yet formulated reasons. Therefore, the teacher must encourage the learners to do so as they go along. Depending on the level of support the teacher gives, this can be done in one of two ways.

First, the teacher can provide examples of language the students might use during the task. For example, in order to present their ideas for alternative uses for the Battersea Power Station task, they may use a range of future forms or modal verbs. Therefore, the teacher might elicit or provide examples such as these:

> We **would** use it as a theatre and music venue.
> We think it **should** be used as a music venue.

In order to encourage learners to formulate the reasons behind the use of these forms, the teacher then asks the following questions:

Why can you use *would* in your presentation?
Why can you use *should*?

Note that rather than using the present progressive in the question, as we saw earlier, the teacher instead uses the modal verb *can*. This is because rather than looking at choices that have already been made, either by the writer of a text or by participants in a dialogue, the learners are now exploring their options for the task ahead. This makes *can* a more suitable modal.

However, as we have seen earlier, it is not necessary to provide useful language models before the task. Instead, the teacher can monitor the preparation stage in order to provide the learners with guidance by inputting useful language or pointing out errors. For example, the teacher may notice learners who want to use the present progressive in their presentations:

We are turning *Battersea Power Station into a theme park.* †

In this instance, the teacher first elicits the fact that this form is not appropriate, as it suggests that the decision has already been made. They then ask the students to reformulate the statement using a more suitable form, for example:

We think they **should turn** *Battersea Power Station into a theme park.*

Once the learners have come up with a more appropriate form, the teacher can then elicit the reason.

As with replication and transposition tasks, the second opportunity the teacher has to explore reasons is after students have completed the task. Here, the same techniques apply. The teacher monitors and notes down examples of interesting, inappropriate or ineffective language. These are then displayed so that the students can explore meanings or reformulate their errors. Once this is done, the teacher can use the following prompts to encourage their learners to formulate reasons or to reflect on what they have done during the lesson:

Why were we using *would* or *should* to do this task?
Why did we use *would* and *should* in this task?

Why L2 learners should explore reasons

This chapter has looked at the ways that teachers can use both text-based and task-based procedures to help learners uncover meanings and formulate reasons. It has also outlined the different techniques that teachers can use in order to encourage their students to do so. However, it is important to note that moving from the use of rules to reasons takes time. Therefore, the last section of this chapter underlines the benefits of making changes to the way we teach by working more with reasons.

Look at these learner-generated reasons and consider them in relation to the benefits of using them, summarised in the points below.

Reason: *The writer is using the present progressive because he sees the situation as unusual. It isn't normally like that.*

1. Where a grammar rule might only be true some of the time, a reason always is. Though a number of writers have suggested that rules do not necessarily have to give the whole truth (eg. Swan, 2006), we have seen in Chapter 2 that unclear or imprecise rules of thumb can often create uncertainty for learners later on. This therefore suggests that truth is at the very least a desirable quality. By helping learners uncover reasons and understand the perspective of the writer or the speaker, this quality is provided much more frequently.

2. 'A rule should answer the question (and only the question) that a student's English is asking' (Swan, 1994), yet if learners are presented with generic rules of thumb that contradict the examples they are exposed to, this will not always be the case. However, if learners are exposed to examples of language in texts and encouraged to ask why the writer or speaker is using a certain form on this specific occasion, the reason that the teacher provides or learners uncover will always answer the question.

Because reasons relate to specific examples of language use, it is important to encourage students to use a progressive form rather than the present simple or imperative. This is also why it is helpful to refer to the speaker or writer rather than using the pronouns *we* and *you*. Analysing reasons and using the progressive form in our descriptions of meaning also enable learners to appreciate how dynamic the language truly is. As Claypole (2011) so eloquently puts it, 'the objective is not to tame the chaos of language but to encourage learners to appreciate the dynamic qualities inherent in its use'. Exploring reasons enables us to do this.

Reason: *Jade is using **used to** to describe Sam's habits when she met him.*

3. Widdowson (1998) suggests that when speakers or writers are communicating, the reader or listener does not ask what the sentences mean but what the people themselves mean. By exploring reasons rather than rules, this is exactly what we are asking our learners to do. Using the speaker's or writer's names in the reasons is an effective way of ensuring that this happens.

4. Exploring reasons encourages learners to make their own discoveries about language use and, by stimulating an investigative approach, 'learners learn how to observe probabilities and tendencies for themselves' (Carter *et al*, 2011). Of course, rule discovery is a technique often used in coursebooks, as it is considered a more engaging, memorable and motivating approach than merely providing learners with explanations. However, coursebook discovery exercises can sometimes be a little *too* guided. This is because what the learners 'discover' has already been decided. More often than not it is a generic rule, and because coursebooks at and around intermediate level tend to cover the same areas of grammar, it is frequently a rule that learners have already come across in a different class or level. This is not really rule discovery; this is the teacher using discovery techniques to elicit declarative knowledge, that is, what the students already know about the language.

However, by focusing on reasons, learners can genuinely enquire about language in any part of a text. All they need to do is ask, 'Why is the writer/speaker using..?' As Willis (2000) puts it, 'knowledge which is gained by one's own efforts is much more likely to stick and to be used than knowledge which is handed over on a plate'. When the knowledge that learners gain is genuinely new, this is discovery in its most meaningful sense.

Reason: *The speaker is using **-ing** because the situation is not normally this way. Usually he hates his job, but in this moment it's ok. †*

5. Rules are not owned by students (Larsen-Freeman, 2003), but reasons are. By encouraging learners to create their own descriptions of meaning and usage, we can give our learners the sense that they are not completely bound by an external set of descriptions that they must comprehend in order to make progress. Instead, they can understand and describe aspects of language in their own words. Indeed, descriptions of meaning do not necessarily have to be in English; the learner can also use their L1. In addition, the creation of a unique, personalised and appropriate description of meaning can be incredibly motivating, as we shall see later in the book.

6. By encouraging learners to create their own descriptions of language use, we also reduce the need for complex grammatical terminology, which not all learners possess. In fact, for some learners it can even be quite alienating.

Reason: *The speaker is using the present perfect simple to say his experience. This is normal in a job interview in the UK. †*

7. As we have seen, rules can be rather prescriptive, as if they exist independently of specific contexts, genres, cultures and routines. However, by looking at reasons, we can help our learners understand how contexts, the genre, the relationship and shared knowledge of the participants all contribute to the way that English speakers frame and understand what they say or write (Swan, 2007). This means that teachers can help learners to better understand the differences between spoken and written language, or to look at the way that language is used in different types of electronic interactions, such as text messages, online forums or tweets. Exploring reasons can also help learners analyse communication undertaken in English as a lingua franca (ELF), an especially relevant goal given the increase in communication across cultures (Meier, 2015).

8. By exploring reasons, learners can discover how language is used to describe facts and show opinions. They can learn how a writer or speaker might use language to persuade, criticise, obscure or stereotype, or how someone might express their culture and identity. As Hymes (1972) suggested, all communicative exchanges are situated in a social context that influences the words and forms that the participants use. Learners

can be helped to see this by exploring reasons; they will not do so just by learning the rules.

Reason: The writer is using the present perfect simple to connect the invention of phones (past) and the effect now.

9. Uncovering reasons is a valuable learning strategy that students can use outside class. As Willis (2000) suggests, 'Learners must make generalisations about the way that the language is formed and used. This not only has the advantage of authenticity, it also develops skills that will make students more self-sufficient when it comes to continuing their linguistic development outside the classroom.' By encouraging our learners to use the stems 'Why is the writer using ... ?' and 'Why is the speaker using ... ?', we empower them by providing a framework. This enables our students to discover the reason underlying whichever grammatical forms they meet (Larsen-Freeman, 2000). Of course, it is important to remember that they may not always be able to come to a satisfactory conclusion. Therefore, teachers need to make themselves available to look at what learners have discovered or surmised. It is not only interesting to see what learners come up with, but the discussions can provide the teacher with ideas and materials for future lessons.

10. An exploration of reasons rather than rules works as a way of training new teachers to develop their language awareness (Bolitho, 2015). This can be very motivating, as it can stop teachers in training from viewing language as a system of complex structures and rules and encourage them to see it as it is: a way of expressing meaning (Norrington-Davies, 2015). Once teachers have uncovered the reasons and created their own descriptions, they can then compare their interpretations with the rules in their coursebook or grammar. Differences or similarities can also be explored in subsequent input sessions or workshops. Encouraging teachers-in-training to uncover reasons also has the positive effect of helping to prevent the issue of new teachers' language awareness becoming coexistent with what they read in coursebooks. This is because they are already developing a necessary degree of criticality and caution.

11. Exploring reasons can help learners and teachers develop more of a 'feel' for the language. Carter *et al* (2011) claim that an exclusive focus on more rule-bound or codified examples of language will not help learners develop this kind of sensitivity, and the same must be true of teachers.

Regardless of how many years' experience a teacher has, they will constantly learn new things about the language. The study of reasons is one way of ensuring that this happens.

Reason: *First the journalist talks about the smuggler. Then he is using the passive so you see it's still about the smuggler.*

12. A focus on reasons helps students reflect on the value of language learning strategies and teaching approaches. At B1 level or higher, a focus on reasons can often lead to interesting discussions on the value and importance of rules. It can also help learners see why it is necessary to be critically evaluative of what they read in their grammars and coursebooks. Opportunities for metacognition such as this enable learners to think more about the learning process, thereby helping to make them more independent in the future. As Ur (2015) suggests, a lot of professional learning is derived from reflecting on experiences, and I believe that this is also true of language learning.

13. Learner-generated reasons can be very memorable and act as prompts or pegs that students go on to use when reconstructing or summarising texts. Whether learner-generated reasons are more memorable than rules is of course open to question and a possible area for research, but the simple fact that they are memorable for some learners is a very positive factor.

14. Widdowson (2003) suggests that 'the acquisition of competence is not accumulative but adaptive: learners proceed not by adding items of knowledge or ability, but by a process of continual revision and reconstruction'. In this regard, a focus on reasons enables teachers to recycle or revisit important areas of language without going over the same set of rules. In fact, a focus on the same language area done in two completely different ways is surely beneficial for the learners, as two modes of input would very possibly create a greater chance that learners will commit the ideas to memory. Widdowson goes on to claim that 'learning is necessarily a process of recurrent unlearning and relearning, whereby encoding rules and conventions for their use are modified, extended, realigned, or abandoned altogether to accommodate new language data'. By focusing on reasons and comparing them with rules, we therefore enable students at higher levels to modify or abandon old ideas to accommodate new ones. This in turn can lead to greater

understanding not only of the language area under consideration but of the rule and the reason that underlie it.

Reason: *We are using 'should' because we believe in our idea. We want to persuade the other students to choose our idea.*

15. The examples that learners analyse do not need to come from texts in the coursebook or those that the teacher brings to class. They can also be generated by students in communicative tasks. During student-to-student interaction, the teacher notes down examples of effective or interesting language use. After they display them for the class, they then ask the learners to explain the reasons behind their use of certain forms. To do this, the teacher uses the frame 'Why are/were you using xxx?' This is effective for two reasons. First, the learners already know what they mean, which makes it easier to describe the reason. The second advantage is that learners are then able to relate form to function. They see that specific language items can be used to do certain things, such as to persuade or promise. They are not just used because the rules make it necessary.

Section 2

1. Teaching resources

Introduction

The photocopiable texts and tasks in this section demonstrate the techniques and principles described in the previous chapters. The first 11 lessons follow a text-based procedure, while the last seven are more task-based. A specific level or range of levels is recommended for each lesson, according to the Common European Framework of Reference (CEFR). All the texts and tasks are suitable for classes of adult or young adult learners, and each one is a standalone lesson. The lessons do not form part of a syllabus and are not meant to be taught in any particular order.

Many of the texts are based on authentic or coursebook materials, while some were written for specific groups of learners studying in the UK. However, each text, task and lesson procedure can be adapted so that it can be made more relevant for different groups of learners and teaching contexts.

Although the texts and tasks have been designed for the language classroom, they can also be used as model lessons on teacher training courses.

How to use the materials

A procedure is provided for each lesson. However, there are no suggested timings for the stages. The length of each stage depends on how much the students engage with the content and what the learners choose to talk about.

- **Lead-in:** Each procedure begins with a suggested lead-in. Lead-ins are designed to engage the learners in the topic of the lesson, provoke curiosity and generate discussion between the students and teacher. At this stage, the focus is on the topic rather than a specific language item.

- **Focus:** In the **text-based lessons**, the procedures come with questions, prompts or tasks that encourage the learners to process the texts for meaning. These prompts do not include traditional comprehension questions. Instead, the questions and tasks are open-ended and designed to stimulate discussion and debate. This means that there are no suggested answers or predetermined outcomes. Instead, the learners are encouraged to draw their own conclusions about what they have read or listened to.

Each lesson contains techniques and prompts that help learners notice specific language items used in the texts or tasks. These language models can be explicit, that is, they can be displayed on the whiteboard or highlighted in the text. Alternatively, learners can be encouraged to look for examples themselves.

- **Task:** In the **task-based lessons**, a **task** replaces the **focus** as the students are not required to read a text or to notice any specific grammatical structures. Instead, this section contains tips on how to prepare for, set up and monitor communicative tasks.

- **Uncovering reasons:** This section outlines techniques the teacher can use to help learners work out why a writer or speaker is using a particular form. For example, a prompt might ask 'Why is the writer using the passive?' or 'Why is the speaker using *would*?'

Think about

In each lesson you will see a section called **Think about**. This is a prompt for you to reflect on the content of the lesson so far and to formulate your own reasons before you use the materials in class. Note that if you are using any of these lessons for training purposes, you could ask the teachers in training to formulate reasons in pairs or small groups and consider how these language items can be further clarified in class.

Further guidance is also provided in the teacher's notes found at the back of the book.

- **Discussing reasons:** Each lesson includes examples of reasons that have been formulated by L2 learners. When you get to these, compare the learners' reasons with the ones you came up with in the **Think about** section. You can also compare these reasons with the rules found in coursebooks or grammars. If there are any differences, consider why this might be the case. Think about which description of language you prefer. If you are using the materials on a teacher training course, ask the teachers-in-training the same question.

In this section, you will also see that some of the learner-generated reasons are grammatically inaccurate. These are indicated with the symbol †. When you get to these, consider how you might reformulate them. Where an error is particularly complicated, interesting or open to interpretation, suggestions for reformulations can be found in the teacher's notes starting on page 181. These are indicated with the symbol ††.

- **Replication and transposition tasks:** Each **text-based lesson** includes suggestions for a replication or transposition task. These tasks are designed to help learners use the new language for communicative purposes. However, each task is open-ended. This means that there are no recommended answers or outcomes. The learners are instead free to use all their language resources in order to complete the task.

- **Sharing work:** In some lessons, there may be a section that includes samples of student work. This is designed to demonstrate possible outcomes to tasks and to provide examples of how learners might use the target language in practice.

- **Feedback loop:** Each lesson concludes with suggested techniques for conducting feedback and exploring learner error.

Teaching tips

Each lesson contains tips for the teacher. These are designed to encourage you to think about possible outcomes of lessons and stages or to discuss the rationale behind specific techniques or prompts. For example, you are encouraged to think how you might provide further clarification of meaning and usage. There are also suggested ideas for follow-up tasks or lessons. This section also provides further rationale for the types of texts, tasks and techniques suggested in the lessons.

Lessons and procedures

	Title	CEFR Level	Language focus
1	The restaurant review	B1	Past simple Present simple Present perfect simple

	Title	CEFR Level	Language focus
2	Jade and Sam	B2+	*used to + infinitive* *be used to + -ing* *get used to + -ing*
3	By the time I get to Phoenix	B1+	*will* for predictions and logical deduction
4	The wild discovery	B1+	The passive
5	The internet ban	B2+	Relative clauses
6	The election pledge	B1 + B2	*will* for promises
7	The sweetshop incident	B2+	*would*
8	A discursive essay	B2 +	Present simple Present continuous Present perfect simple
9	School rules	A2 + B1	Modals of obligation
10	Cheese rolling and wife carrying	B1 + B2	Present simple
11	Student dilemmas	B1	Conditionals
12	The magic camera	A2+	Narrative tenses
13	The ranking task	A2+	Ways of expressing facts and opinions
14	The balloon debate	A2+	Ways of expressing opinions and arguments
15	The go-between	B1+	Reported speech
16	The job interview	B1+	Various forms
17	What happened?	A2+	Using speculative language
18	Battersea Power Station	B1+	*would* *should* *going to and will*

Lesson 1: The restaurant review

In this lesson, learners read a restaurant review and uncover the reasons why the writer is using the past simple, present simple and the present perfect simple.

Before intermediate level, it is common for these three forms to be introduced in coursebooks in separate units, with the present simple often introduced before the past simple. The present perfect simple is then looked at much later. However, this means that learners can end up waiting for quite a long time in their development before they see how these tenses interact in longer and more authentic stretches of discourse.

The following text and lesson procedure is designed to enable learners to explore all three forms at a fairly early stage. It is also designed to help learners see that where the past simple is used to indicate time, the present simple describes general truths. There is no actual focus on time. This is a useful distinction for students to make.

EatoutLondon   Casablanca

I often take friends and family to this authentic Moroccan restaurant and have lost count of how many times I've been here. The owners have succeded in creating an intimate and friendly atmosphere where you almost feel as though you are dining in someone's home. You can also watch the food being prepared just a few feet away from your table. Along with the smells, colours and flavours, this really makes you feel like you're on holiday.

I always have the sharing meze and cold salads to start. These come with an amazing mix of flavours, textures and colours and it's beautifully presented too. I think I've tried all the main dishes on the menu, which is lucky as it's always difficult to choose what to have. On my last visit I went for the lamb, which was unbelievable. The meat dishes here are always done to perfection, the couscous or rice is light and fluffy and the servings are really generous. I recommend you finish every meal with the cardamom ice cream and a good glass of piping hot mint tea. You'll feel great afterwards.

If you want to drink alcohol, then you have to bring your own but they don't charge for corkage. You also have to remember that they only take cash and the nearest machine is back at the station. It's also best to make a reservation if you want to be sure to get a table. This place is super-popular, particularly on weekends, although I've been lucky enough to get a table without waiting on some occasions. If you are in a hurry, then Casablanca is probably not for you. However, if you like great food that takes time to prepare and you want to experience a taste of North Africa, then there isn't a better place to eat.

Kathy

Overall rating ★ ★ ★ ★ ★ ★ ★ ★ ★ ★

Food 10 | Service 9 | Atmosphere 9 | Value for money 9

Friday, May 04, 2015

This lesson includes a simple replication activity in which the learners write their own restaurant review. To make this task more challenging, you can encourage learners to post their reviews on well-known websites such as Trip Advisor or London-eating.com. As a student, getting your work published on a website can be extremely motivating. It can make students feel better about their writing, hopefully encouraging them to do more. Writing more reviews will also provide plenty of creative and meaningful practice of the three important forms found in the text.

Lesson procedure

Lead-in: Students can talk about restaurants they have been to and share good and bad experiences. Alternatively, students brainstorm what they would find in a restaurant review. Discuss why people read restaurant reviews and where they are found.

Focus: The students read Kathy's review of the restaurant and discuss whether it is positive or negative. Ask if the review would make them want to eat there or not. Allow plenty of time to explore ideas and emerging language.

Teaching tips

Does the review make you want to eat at this restaurant? Why/why not?

A genuine question such as this is particularly effective as it encourages the learners to read the text for the purpose it was written. It is also useful to tell the students that they can use this question every time they read a review, whether it is for a restaurant, film or play. By encouraging the students to recycle this question, we provide them with the tools to read more extensively outside class and to gain a better understanding of this particular genre.

Uncovering reasons: Display the three model sentences below. Ask the students why Kathy is using the following forms:

These <u>come</u> with an amazing mix of flavours and <u>it's beautifully presented</u> too.
On my last visit <u>I went for the lamb</u>.
I think <u>I've tried everything</u> on the menu.

Think about

Before the lesson, try to formulate your own reasons for the examples above. How do they compare with the reasons below, formulated by a group of students at B1 level?

Kathy is using present simple to describe <u>anyone's</u> visit at any time. If you go now it's the same and if you go in the future it's the same.

Kathy is using past simple to describe <u>her</u> last visit on Saturday. It's just one visit.

Past simple for one visit, present simple for always. Present perfect for all <u>her</u> visits in the past to now.

How can you use the reasons above to further clarify how the three forms are used within the text? Note how the past simple and the present perfect simple are used to describe Kathy's visits, while the present simple is actually more general. It is used to describe her feelings about the restaurant, but also to tell future customers what to expect.

Discussing reasons: Explore learner-generated reasons in feedback.

Replication activity: The learners write a review of their favourite restaurant or a restaurant they have recently been to. Alternatively, they could write a review of an invented restaurant. It is useful before this stage to give the learners time to prepare and think about what they want to include in their review.

Sharing work: The learners share their reviews, perhaps by displaying them around the classroom or working in small groups. As in the reading stage, ask the students to decide if the review would make them want to eat in the restaurant, in order to give them a purpose for reading each other's texts.

Feedback loop: Display or distribute examples of interesting or incorrect language for analysis. Remember to use the frame *Why are you using …? or Why did you use …?* to encourage learners to focus on their use of specific forms.

Lesson 2: Jade and Sam

This text and guided discovery activity from *Speakout Upper Intermediate* (Eales & Oakes, 2011) is designed to demonstrate how *used to* and *would* can be used to describe past habits. It also contains examples of *be used to*, which is used to talk about events and actions that are familiar, and *get used to*, which shows how these things become more familiar over time.

It's like a drug …

JADE'S STORY

When I first met Sam I really liked him. He was good-looking and kind but quite shy. He **used to play computer games** – one in particular – quite a lot. I'd visit him at his home and <u>he'd be sitting</u> in front of his computer. Sometimes he didn't even turn round, and I thought it was strange but <u>I soon got used to talking to his back</u>. Anyway, three years ago we got married.

Now when he comes home from work, one of us cooks dinner, while the other one looks after our son, Joe. Then instead of sitting down and chatting about the day, Sam usually goes straight to his computer to play *Battle Galaxy 2525*. Whenever I try to get him to watch a movie on TV or something, he usually completely ignores me or he agrees and then gets bored because he wants to go back to his game. <u>I'm not used to that type of behaviour</u>. It's very different from my family. I feel ignored and often ask myself why I stay with this guy.

It wouldn't be so bad if it was just me. But whenever his parents come round he carries on playing and ignores them. Sometimes he turns round to say something but he often doesn't know what we've been talking about. So I have to talk to them and pretend that everything is normal.

I remember once I got really annoyed and unplugged his computer. He was furious – he said I'd killed some of his 'friends'. I think these 'virtual' friends are more important to him than me and Joe. I mean they aren't even real! I couldn't believe it. I shouted at him that he only thinks of himself and his virtual world … we didn't talk to each other for a whole week.

And Joe? I suppose <u>he's used to his father being on the computer</u> because he's never known anything different. But Sam's idea of being a good father is showing Joe how to tap on the computer keyboard. One thing's for sure,

I'm never going to let Joe start playing computer games. I've threatened to leave Sam but it would be terrible for Joe. I'm sure that deep down Sam knows he's in the wrong. It's like a drug. I think he needs help.

Rules:

a) Use *used to* to talk about activities and states which *happen regularly in the present/happened in the past but not usually now.*

b) Use *would* to talk about *activities/states* in the past which no longer happen now.

c) Use *be used to* to talk about things that are *familiar/strange* to us.

d) Use *get used to* to talk about things that *are familiar/become familiar to us over a period of time.*

e) After *used to* and *would*, use the *infinitive/the -ing form or a noun.*

f) After *be used to* and *get used to*, use *the infinitive/the -ing form or a noun.*

© Speakout Upper Intermediate. (Pearson, 2011)

As well as being engaging and capable of generating a lot of debate and discussion, this text also contains an interesting and unusual example of *used to* (line 2 in the text, in bold). Usually, this form describes past habits that no longer continue into the present. However, in this text, the writer is using it to describe a habit that still continues in the present. This 'exception to the rule' makes this a very appropriate text for exploring reasons, as it can extend the learners' knowledge and understanding of this common language point.

Lesson procedure

Lead-in: Display the title 'It's like a drug' and ask the students to guess what the article might be about. Allow time to explore the learners' ideas. The students read the text to see if their ideas were correct.

Focus: The students read the text again and answer the question, 'Why did she marry him?' This question encourages the learners to interact with the text and think more deeply about Jade and Sam's relationship. It also encourages the learners to think about Jade's possible reasons for writing the text. Allow plenty of time in feedback to explore ideas and emerging language.

Uncovering reasons: Display the four model sentences below. Ask the learners why Jade is using the following forms:

He <u>used to play</u> computer games quite a lot.
I'<u>d visit</u> him at his home and he'd be sitting at the computer.
I soon <u>got used to talking</u> to his back.
I'<u>m not used to</u> that type of behaviour.

Think about

Before the lesson, try to formulate your own reasons for the examples above. How do they compare with the reasons below, formulated by a group of students at B2 level?

*Jade is using **used to** to describe Sam's habits when she met him.*

*Jade is using **used to** to describe Sam's habits before they got married.*

*Jade is using got **used to** describe strange before but now it's normal for Jade. †*

*Jade is using **I'm not used** to to show it is strange behaviour for her.*

How can you use the reasons above to clarify how *used to* can describe a past habit that continues to the present? Note that this is only possible if something else has changed between the past and now. In this case, it is Jade and Sam's circumstances.

Discussing reasons: Explore the learner-generated reasons in feedback.

Replication activity: The learners rewrite the story from Sam's perspective, using the prompt *When I first met Jade ....* As they write their stories, monitor and help with any difficulties.

Sharing work: The learners share their stories with the class.

Feedback loop: Display or distribute examples of interesting or incorrect language for analysis. Remember to use the frame *Why are you using ...?* or *Why did you use ...?* to encourage learners to focus on their use of specific forms.

Teaching tips

Look at the following examples taken from the replication task. Note how the learners have used the target language to create some interesting and amusing examples. However, because there is a lot of freedom in the task, it means that unexpected language issues can occur. Look at the example underlined below. Do you think this example is correct or not?

- *I used to play computer games before we got married, so I don't know what her problem is.*
- *She would come to my home and she'd be sitting behind me when I was playing games.*
- *Unfortunately we got married, but I soon got used to her strange behaviour.*

Though perfectly acceptable, this use of *would be + verb + -ing* has the potential to confuse students. See the teacher's notes for suggestions on how you could demonstrate the possible difference between *would + base form* and *would be + verb + -ing*.

Lesson 3: By the time I get to Phoenix

In this lesson, learners listen to 'By the time I get to Phoenix' by Glen Campbell and uncover the reason why the singer is using will + infinitive and will be + -ing (commonly called the future simple and the future continuous).

One thing to bear in mind before this lesson is the fact that in many coursebooks, *going to* is said to describe predictions with strong evidence while will signifies less certainty. However, Parrott (2010) suggests that in its contracted form, *will* expresses logical deduction. This is nicely demonstrated in this song.

'By the time I get to Phoenix'

By the time I get to Phoenix she'll be rising
She'll find the note I left hangin' on her door
She'll laugh when she reads the part that says I'm leavin'
'Cause I've left that girl so many times before

By the time I make Albuquerque she'll be working
She'll prob'ly stop at lunch and give me a call
But she'll just hear that phone keep on ringin'
Off the wall that's all

Continued

> ### By the Time I get to Phoenix (continued)
>
> By the time I make Oklahoma she'll be sleepin'
> She'll turn softly and call my name out low
> And she'll cry just to think I'd really leave her
> Tho' time and time I try to tell her so
> She just didn't know I would really go.
>
> **Words and music by Jimmy Webb**

The song can also be used to set up a very engaging and creative replication activity, as can be seen below.

Lesson procedure

Lead-in: Display a map of the USA and ask students to discuss why someone might drive from one coast the other. It is also useful to pre-teach Phoenix, Albuquerque and Oklahoma.

Focus:

■ The students listen to the song and work out why the singer is driving away from Phoenix (he is leaving his partner). Encourage the students to speculate why this might be the case.

■ Ask the students to discuss how they feel about the singer's actions. Allow plenty of time to explore ideas and language that emerge from this discussion.

Uncovering reasons: Encourage the learners to notice the examples of *will* in the text. Ask the learners why the singer is using *will* + infinitive and *will be* + *-ing* in the following examples:

> *By the time I get to Phoenix, <u>she'll be rising</u>.*
> *<u>She'll find</u> the note I left hangin' on her door.*

Discussing reasons: Explore the learner-generated reasons in feedback.

Replication activity: Give the students the prompt, *By the time I get to Pittsburgh …* or *By the time he gets to Pittsburgh …* . The learners write a fourth verse of the song, taking either the singer's or his partner's perspective. As they write their verses, monitor and help with any difficulties.

Sharing work: The learners share their new verses, perhaps by reading them out or displaying them around the room. Perhaps they can even have a go at singing them.

Feedback loop: Display or distribute examples of interesting or incorrect language for analysis. Remember to use the frame *Why are you using …?* or *Why did you use …?* to encourage learners to focus on their use of specific forms.

Teaching tips

This is a simple, engaging and fun follow-up task. It not only allows for creativity but is also very open-ended, as students can either continue to follow the rhythm of the song or write their version in prose. Consider also how you might deal with some of the emerging issues with lexis, for example, the difference between *listen to* and *hear*, and the use of *cut in* the following examples.

By the time I get to Pittsburgh she'll be partying
She'll listen to our song and start to cry ††

By the time I get to Pittsburgh, she'll still be crying
She'll take my clothes out of the closet and burn them
She'll cut all my pictures and letters ††

I'll forget his name and our life before. Also, I'll move to the Caribbean with my new man. We'll be sunbathing, eating lobster and drinking ice-cold champagne with strawberries.

Lesson 4: The wild discovery

ELT coursebooks frequently introduce new language items through graded texts. They also commonly use a technique known as 'input flooding', whereby a text deliberately contains a high number of examples of the target language item. This is designed to increase the chances of learners noticing the items.

The article below is intended to resemble the kind of graded text found in intermediate and upper-intermediate coursebooks. In this case, it has been designed to introduce and analyse the passive voice, of which there are 10 examples in the text (one is a reduced form). Once the learners have read the text and discussed the content, it is usual for coursebooks to then include a guided discovery activity. This generally leads students towards the common rule stating that the passive is used when the speaker is not known or not important. However, as we saw in Chapter 2, this rule is not entirely correct. By encouraging learners to focus on the role of the writer and by looking for reasons rather than rules, L2 learners are capable of uncovering something closer to the truth.

Police make wild discovery in airport luggage

A 50-year-old shopkeeper <u>has been arrested</u> at a UK airport for attempting to bring body parts, bones and eggs from a range of protected species into the country in his luggage. After <u>being stopped and questioned</u> by airport police and customs officials, a shop belonging to the man <u>was searched</u> and various illegal items <u>were seized</u> and <u>taken away</u> for testing. Amongst a large haul of uncertified items, police found turtle shells and eggs as well as bottles of snake wine, a drink <u>believed</u> in many parts of Asia to have restorative and curative powers.

The suspect claimed that he had bought the illegal objects for his private collection and as gifts. Although police found a number of additional items in a storeroom behind the shop, the man has claimed that they have nothing to do with his business and <u>are not offered</u> for sale.

The accused, who <u>cannot be named</u> until the investigation is complete, <u>has been released</u> on bail until a court date <u>can be set</u>.

Lesson procedure

Lead-in: Display the headline 'Police make wild discovery in airport luggage' and ask the students to guess what the article might be about. Allow time to explore the learners' ideas.

Focus:

- The students read the text quickly to see if their ideas were correct.

- The students read the text again and answer the question 'What punishment should the man get?' This question encourages the learners to interact with the text and offer opinions about the seriousness of the offence. Allow plenty of time in feedback to explore ideas and opinions.

- Noticing activity: The students read the text again and underline examples of the passive. Alternatively, examples of the passive could already be highlighted in the text.

Uncovering reasons: Display some of the examples from the text. Ask the students why the journalist is using the passive in the following examples:

A 50-year-old shopkeeper <u>has been arrested</u> at a UK airport …
A shop belonging to the man <u>was searched</u> and various illegal items <u>were seized</u> …
The accused <u>has been released</u> on bail until a trial date <u>can be set</u>.

Think about

Before the lesson, try to formulate your own reasons for the use of the passive in the examples above. How do they compare with the reasons below, formulated by a group of students at B2 level?

Because first he introduce the man then he wants to keep focus on the man. ††

First he talks about the smugglers. Then he is using the passive so you see it's still about the smuggler.

He talks first about the man so it's the man, the man, the man.

During the language focus stage, it is useful to encourage students to consider the role of the journalist and why they may have chosen to make the suspect the main focus of the article. See the teacher's notes on page 183 for suggestions.

Discussing reasons: Explore the learner-generated reasons in feedback.

Replication activity: Using the headline as a prompt, the students reconstruct the article from memory. To make this easier, the students could be given key words as prompts. Alternatively, give the students a different headline. They then have to write their own article.

Sharing work: The learners share their new stories, perhaps by reading them out to the whole class or displaying them around the classroom.

Feedback loop: Display or distribute examples of interesting or incorrect language for analysis. Remember to use the frame *Why are you using …?* or *Why did you use …?* to encourage learners to focus on their use of specific forms.

Teaching tips

At higher levels, it is a good idea to use this procedure with more authentic texts or current news reports. It is also a good idea to encourage students to find other examples of the passive in news reports to see if it is being used for the same reasons as the ones uncovered in this lesson.

Lesson 5: The internet ban

Martin Parrott (2010) suggests that 'long before we expect or require our learners to use relative clauses, we can help them to recognise and understand them by systematically drawing their attention to how and why they are used in genuine texts'. This is what the following lesson sets out to do. However, rather than helping learners to understand the use of relative clauses by looking at how they work in a text (Text A), this lesson explores what happens when they are taken away (Text B).

As it is perhaps unrealistic to then expect learners to try to use relative clauses in a freer, communicative task, this lesson does not include a replication task. Instead, we will see how the content of the following text can act as a stimulus for a fun and creative transposition task.

Text A: Village at war over internet ban	Text B: Village at war over internet ban
Haversham, **a picturesque village in the South of England, known locally for its cream teas and country walks**, has found itself at the centre of a storm, reports Gabriel Winston	Haversham has found itself at the centre of a storm, reports Gabriel Winston
A controversial new 'law' has been passed that stops children under the age of 17 from using the internet in public places, despite the opposition of teachers, youth groups and some small business. The ban, **which covers cafes, libraries and the local secondary and primary schools**, will come into effect in July 2016, nine years after smoking was banned in public. In addition to public places, children will be barred from accessing Wi-Fi in the community centre and student common rooms at the local sixth form college.	A controversial new 'law' has been passed that stops children under the age of 17 from using the internet in public places, despite the opposition of teachers, youth groups and some small business. The ban will come into effect in July 2016, nine years after smoking was banned in public. In addition to public places, children will be barred from accessing Wi-Fi in the community centre and student common rooms at the local sixth form college.
The law, **which was unanimously passed by the town council**, was first proposed by Mrs Marjorie Simpkins, **Mayor of Haversham for the past 32 years**. 'The internet is a terrible, corrupting influence on our young people. It encourages	The law was first proposed by Mrs Marjorie Simpkins. 'The internet is a terrible, corrupting influence on our young people. It encourages them to spend their days posting inane or

them to spend their days posting inane or insulting messages, sharing pointless gossip or rotting their brains with violent games. This has to stop before we produce a generation of mindless zombies unable to string a sentence together or communicate face to face'. The mayor, **who has previously called for age restrictions on Facebook and Twitter**, went on to call the internet 'the defining issue of the age'.	insulting messages, sharing pointless gossip or rotting their brains with violent games. This has to stop before we produce a generation of mindless zombies unable to string a sentence together or communicate face to face'. The mayor went on to call the internet 'the defining issue of the age'.
Her views were echoed by many local residents. Kate Demaine, **who voted in favour of the law**, claimed that using the internet 'has encouraged children to stop thinking for themselves', while many expressed concerns about online bullying.	Her views were echoed by many local residents. Kate Demaine claimed that using the internet 'has encouraged children to stop thinking for themselves', while many expressed concerns about online bullying.
However, not all residents support the ban. Carl Anderson, **cafe owner and caretaker at the local community centre**, believes that young people will end up going to places where he or parents will be unable to keep an eye on their children or keep them safe, while Terry Halsome, **the local librarian**, strongly opposes the ban. 'The Library is full of young people now we have computers and internet access,' he claimed. 'The kids **who come here** don't just sit around all day playing games and going on social media. They're studying and learning new things. A ban will take that away from them'. A meeting at the Town Hall is scheduled for today.	However, not all residents support the ban. Carl Anderson believes that young people will end up going to places where he or parents will be unable to keep an eye on their children or keep them safe, while Terry Halsome strongly opposes the ban. 'The Library is full of young people now we have computers and internet access,' he claimed. 'The kids don't just sit around all day playing games and going on social media. They're studying and learning new things. A ban will take that away from them'. A meeting at the Town Hall is scheduled for today.

Lesson procedure

Lead-in: Show pictures of a traditional English village. Ask the students to predict why this village might be in the news.

Focus:

- The students read Text A to see if their ideas were correct.

- The students read Text A again. They discuss why the adults in the village might want to ban young people from using the internet in public spaces and what will happen if the ban goes ahead. The students can also discuss what they would do if this happened in their home towns or cities.

- Hand out Text B. The students read the text and discuss why Text B is harder to follow.

Uncovering reasons: Highlight examples of relative clauses in the text. Ask the learners why <u>the writer</u> is using them and how they help the reader understand the text.

The ban was first proposed by Marjorie Simpkins,
<u>Mayor of Haversham for the past 32 years</u>.
Terry Halsame, <u>the local librarian</u>, believes that young people <u>will ...</u>
'<u>The kids who come here</u> don't just sit around all day playing games ...'

Think about

Before the lesson, try to formulate your own reasons for the examples above. How do they compare with the reasons below, formulated by a group of students at B2 level?

If the writer doesn't say it [the relative clause] the reader doesn't know who some of the people are.

Take it [the relative clause] out and we're lost for a moment. We don't know who it is.

The man says it's not all the kids it's only part of the kids in the library ... ††

Discussing reasons: Explore the learner-generated reasons in feedback.

In each of the examples under **Uncovering reasons**, omitting the relative clause would momentarily cause some confusion for the reader, as the students have recognised. However, this is not always the case. To demonstrate this, ask the students to formulate a reason for the use of the relative clause in the following example:

The mayor, <u>who has previously called for restrictions on Facebook and Twitter</u>, went on to say that the internet was 'the defining issue of the age'.

Think about

Look at the reason below, formulated by the same group of learners.

We don't need to know this information but now we know more about her character and history.

How does this reason compare with the following rule, which is frequently found in intermediate and upper intermediate coursebooks?

■ A non-defining relative clause provides extra, non-essential information about a person or thing.

First, the reason is more specific. It also demonstrates that students at B2 level are able to appreciate that non-defining relative clauses can do much more than simply provide 'extra information'. At times, they can actually help us understand who someone is and how they think. This is a useful area to explore.

Transposition task: The students perform a role play of a meeting at the town hall. Distribute the role cards below and give students time to prepare their arguments. When the students are ready, start the meeting.

Terry Halsome, librarian from Haversham

You are opposed to any ban on using the internet. You feel that young people are using the library more and more and see many benefits of this. As well as this, you feel the internet is a good learning tool. Before you join the debate, think of two more reasons for opposing the ban.

Carl Anderson, cafe owner and caretaker of the community centre

You do not support a ban on using the internet. You are worried that this will drive young people away and put them in danger in places outside the village. You also have internet facilities at the community centre, which has made the place more popular than ever before. Before you join the debate, think of two more reasons for opposing the ban.

William Rees, parent and resident of Haversham

Although you do not really know how to use the internet, you are worried that a ban will make your children spend too much time at home and that you will be forced to regulate their internet time. You are also worried that they will find other, more dangerous things to do outside the village. Before you join the debate, think of two more reasons for opposing the ban.

Omar Afridi, resident of Haversham

You and your wife moved to the village four years ago when she was expecting her first child. You now have two young children, and you commute to London three days a week for your work in IT support. You cannot believe that the people of the village think the ban is a good idea. You feel the internet is an educational tool and a way to communicate with the world. You think you would rather raise a young person in London than keep them in a village with such an old-fashioned outlook. Before you join the debate, think of two more reasons for introducing the ban.

Marjorie Simpkins, Mayor of Haversham

You are, of course, in favour of a ban on using the internet in public places. You feel it is making children mindless zombies who cannot speak properly or communicate face-to-face. Before you join the debate, think of two more reasons for introducing the ban.

Kate Demaine, parent and resident of Haversham

You support the ban because you are worried that the internet stops young people from thinking for themselves. You are also concerned about online bullying. Before you join the debate, think of two more reasons for introducing the ban.

Stephanie Charlton-Harrington, Head Teacher of Haversham Primary school

You were opposed to the introduction of computers at the school and you feel they have made the place worse. You are sad that children never seem to spend time outside or make things with their hands anymore. They just spend all day playing video games and emailing their friends. You also feel you would have more control if the internet was banned. Before you join the debate, think of two more reasons for introducing the ban.

Chris Jones, local police officer

You are worried that the internet is increasing instances of violent behaviour. You are also concerned that young people might use it for hacking or tricking older people out of their money, or that they may be scammed themselves. Before you join the debate, think of two more reasons for introducing the ban.

Feedback loop: Display or distribute examples of interesting or incorrect language for analysis. Remember to use the frame *Why are you using …?* or *Why did you use …?* to encourage learners to focus on their use of specific forms.

Lesson 6: The election pledge

YouTube is full of videos of politicians making short speeches and election pledges, and these can be the stimulus for interesting and lively lessons.

A key consideration is choosing which speech or speeches to use. For example, if an election in an English-speaking country is approaching, the teacher can use pledges given by the main candidates, as in the speech given below by Ed Miliband, the former leader of the UK Labour Party, before the 2015 general election (this speech can be viewed at: https://youtu.be/sWW gtVdeGso?list=PL7TD3AB3khUHB0FRlTd24HX_8Xiwl6qE2). This makes the topic more contemporary and relevant, especially for students studying in that particular country. However, even if an election is not imminent, historical speeches can work just as well.

The teacher also has to consider whether to use a speech that contains policies that the learners will agree with or whether to use one with less popular ideas. There is also the option of using two speeches and encouraging learners to think about which policies they prefer and which speaker they would vote for.

So we will legislate in the first year of a Labour government for a fair deal for those who rent. And we're going to oversee also a revolution in home ownership in this country. There'll be the biggest house-building programme for a generation. We'll build at least 200,000 homes a year by the end of the parliament, on course to start building one million new homes. We'll unlock five billion pounds for a future homes fund to help build those new homes. We'll build a new generation of towns, garden cities and suburbs.

And we won't let large developers just hoard land. We know what happens. They wait for it to go up in value, when it could be used to build homes. We'll say either you use the land … or you lose the land. And as we've laid out, new housing will be our first priority for capital investment, including for council housing and housing associations.

But friends we won't just build homes. We'll make sure there is real priority for first-time buyers. It is simply too expensive for so many young people to build … to buy a home today: saving up for the deposit, paying the fees, having enough left over for stamp duty. So we're going to act. We're going to put first-time buyers first. For the first three years of the next Labour government, we will abolish stamp duty for all first-time buyers buying a home under £300,000.

©Sky news Ltd. 27 April 2015

The following lesson procedure is designed to enable learners at B1 and B2 to explore how the modal verb *will* is used by politicians to make pledges and promises and to convince people to vote for them. It is also designed to develop students' listening skills by raising awareness of features of connected speech, and the students get useful and motivating speaking practice by using what they have learnt to make their own election speeches. This lesson has another interesting outcome, as it can help the teacher see what their students might feel about the school or the classes. This can lead on to a useful discussion about what the students like or don't like about the school, and what changes, if any, they would like to see made.

Lesson procedure

Lead-in: Show pictures of politicians and ask the students to brainstorm the kinds of things they say in election speeches. To encourage debate and discussion, ask the students if they believe the promises that politicians make.

Focus: The students listen to the politician's speech and note down what he or she promises to deliver. To encourage students to engage with the topic and really think about the content, ask why the politician is making these pledges and why they may be popular. You can also ask the students if they would vote for these policies or not.

Teaching tips

At B1 and B2, authentic listening texts such as political speeches can be challenging for learners. However, using short authentic recordings presents an opportunity for students to develop rather than merely practise their listening skills. This means that as well as encouraging students to listen for meaning (top-down processing) listening activities should also help them develop decoding skills. This means listening for individual sounds or words, identifying sentence stress or weak forms, or marking the chunks of meaning or pauses in the recording. This is known as decoding or bottom-up processing.

Therefore, after students have listened to the speeches and explored their meaning, it is a good idea to give the students the transcript and do some decoding work. In this lesson, the students can begin by marking where the politician pauses. They can then identify which words carry the main stresses. This can be done either as they listen or after they have predicted where they think the stress will fall.

This stage not only develops listening skills and raises awareness of features of connected speech. It will also help the learners when they come to make their own speeches in the replication task.

Uncovering reasons: Display pledges from the recording you use. Ask the students why the politician is using *will + infinitive* in their pledges.

> *There'll be the biggest house-building programme for a generation.*
> *We'll build at least 200,000 homes a year by the end of the parliament.*
> *We'll build a new generation of towns, garden cities and suburbs.*

Think about

Before the lesson, try to formulate your own reasons for the examples above. How do they compare with the reasons below, formulated by a group of students at B1 level?

*He is using **will** because he is making promises. He wants people to vote for him.*

*He is using **will** because he can make the changes. He has power and possibility. ††*

He's not imagining. He is promising.

At this stage, it is a good idea to look again at where the stress falls in each pledge. Drill the phrases so that students get practice stressing the prominent words before they do the replication activity. In this particular speech, it would also be useful to explore how the speaker uses going to and will for the same reason.

Discussing reasons: Explore learner-generated reasons in feedback.

Replication activity: Split the students into pairs or small groups. Tell the students that the school needs a new principal and one is going to be chosen through an election. Each candidate must create their own policies and deliver them in a speech. Give students plenty of time to prepare. As you monitor, encourage students to mark which words they will emphasise in their speeches and encourage them to practise.

Sharing work: The students perform their pledges. Once everyone has had a turn, ask the class to vote for the best policies. They cannot vote for themselves.

Feedback loop: Display or distribute examples of interesting or incorrect language for analysis, such as those below. Remember to use the frame *Why are you using …?* or *Why did you use …?* to encourage learners to focus on their use of specific forms.

Classes will begin at 10am and the coffee break will be extended by 10 minutes. We will build a cinema in the school, so students can watch films together. The students can drink coffee during the lesson. ††

Lesson 7: The sweet shop incident

I enjoy telling stories and anecdotes in class and I try to encourage my students to do the same. I don't know when I first told this story, but it is one that students have always responded to positively. This could be due to the fact that people generally relate to stories about childhood. However, I also believe that the act of storytelling builds the relationship between me and the students and helps them to see me outside the role of language teacher.

Ok, so I <u>would've been about eight or nine</u> and me, my brother and sister and my two cousins we were staying with my grandmother for the summer holidays. She lived in a village called East Hoathly, and there was this old-fashioned sweet shop there where they kept the sweets in jars on shelves behind the counter. This meant that the old lady who ran the place had to climb a step ladder to get to them. Anyway, because she wasn't very nice and scared us a bit, we invented a bit of a mean game. We'd go in and choose some sweets from one side of the room, and the little old lady had to move the ladder and climb up and get them. Then we'd make her go to a different shelf and climb up the ladder again. And we'd do this over and over. No wonder she didn't like us.

After a while we realised that while the lady was climbing the ladder, she couldn't see the sweets and chocolates on the counter, so I'm ashamed to say that we started to pinch them. And not just once or twice. It became part of the game.

Anyway, one day my brother and my cousin, who were both a couple of years older than me, dared me to go to the shop and steal some sweets. So I went in there as normal and got the old lady climbing up and down the ladder and managed to pinch some sweets. So I started going back the park where the others were, but as I was walking over this bridge by the stream, I suddenly had a moment of realisation, and I stopped, and I said to myself, 'This is really bad. We're stealing! Stealing's bad.' So I did the only sensible thing and I threw all the sweets into the stream. I then started walking to the park again, but just a second or two later, I had another realisation. 'They're not going to believe me! They're going to think I didn't do it!' And because I was so worried that they'd think I'd chickened out, I went back.

So I went back into the shop, got the old lady to climb up the ladder, and rather than just buy some sweets, I tried to nick some. But I guess she was a bit suspicious, because as I was putting some sweets in my pocket, she turned round and caught me.

It was horrible. The old lady didn't call the police. She did something much worse. She called my granny who came to the shop to get me. It was awful. She didn't shout at me or send me to my room, but every time she looked at me she looked so disappointed. She also made me write a letter of apology and take it to the old lady and I had to phone my mum and dad and tell them what I'd done. The worst thing was I had to take the punishment all alone because I couldn't sneak on the others. And that was it for the rest of the summer. My granny doing everything as normal, but always looking at me as if she was really disappointed.

It's funny to think that if I hadn't had a pang of conscience, I wouldn't have been caught, but I quickly learned that I really shouldn't have done it in the first place. I have my grandmother to thank for that.

This lesson can be used with students from B1 to C2 level. As well as providing useful listening practice and giving learners the opportunity to tell anecdotes and share memories, this story can also help learners explore narrative tenses and storytelling techniques. However, I often use it to help the learners uncover different uses of the modal verb *would*.

Lesson procedure

Lead-in: I use a picture of myself at the age I was in the story and the students guess what I was like.

Focus: Tell the students the story. Tell them they can stop you at any time for clarification or questions. For lower level students, you can provide some support by displaying pictures depicting the story, for example, a traditional sweet shop, a packet of chewy sweets, a grumpy old lady, a river, a child being told off. The students look at the pictures and try to guess what happened in the story. If you're going to tell your own story, tell the students that they can ask you questions as you go along.

Teaching tips

Live listening simply means that rather than listen to a recording, the students listen to a teacher or a visitor to the classroom. There are a number of benefits of using this technique in class. First, as long as the speaker does not read directly from a script, the learner is exposed to genuine, real-time language with examples of incompleteness, false starts and hesitations. Because learners are able to interact and ask for clarification, they are also involved in genuine, real-time communication. This can also help learners develop listening and speaking strategies, such as asking for clarification. The use of eye-contact, gesture and facial expressions also makes them feel more involved in the task.

Live listening can also be incredibly motivating and engaging. This is because students around the world seem to love learning more about their teachers. This is why I tell a story about doing something naughty and stupid. My students seem to enjoy it and find it memorable. What would your story be?

Uncovering reasons: Display the four model sentences below. The learners uncover why I am using *would* in the following sentences.

I *would have been* about eight or nine …
We'd make her go to a different shelf and climb up the ladder again.
I was so worried *they'd think* I'd chickened out …
If I hadn't had a pang of conscience I *wouldn't have been* caught …

Think about

Before you teach the lesson, try to formulate your own reasons for the examples above. How do they compare with the reasons below, formulated by a group of students at B1 level?

You're saying your age more or less in the story. You don't know exactly.

You made the old lady do this again and again. You didn't do it only once.

You suppose what your brother will do if you don't bring the sweets. But in the story it's past so it's **would** *not* **will**. †

It happened the other way and you regret this way. You wish it happened another way. †

Discovering reasons: Explore learner-generated reasons in feedback.

Replication task: If you want to do a focused task, the students can work in pairs to reconstruct the story from prompts. This can be done either as a written or spoken task. For a free, more unfocused task, the learners can share their own anecdote about a memorable childhood experience.

Sharing work: Once learners have reconstructed the text, put them into small groups to compare their versions.

Feedback loop: Explore some of the target language and interesting language emerging from their texts. Remember to use the frame *Why are you using xxx here?* to encourage students to focus on their use of specific forms. Remember that if you are doing an unfocused task, the students may not necessarily use *would*. Therefore, you can use feedback to explore where it was possible to do so.

Lesson 8: A discursive essay

Students hoping to pass English examinations such as the Cambridge Advanced Exam (CAE) or the IELTS test will need to write a discursive essay. In this task, learners typically have between 180 and 250 words to present a balanced and objective discussion of a subject or to argue in support of or against a proposition. Alternatively, learners may be asked to consider both sides of an argument or present advantages and disadvantages. The writer then completes the essay by summarising what they have written or drawing tentative conclusions about the topic.

There are a number of sound reasons for training learners to write discursive essays, First, a great deal of the writing that learners are required to do at school and university is discursive in nature. As we have seen above, many English language examinations include a discursive essay. Even if learners do not plan to take exams or go on to university, reading and writing discursive texts helps learners to develop and organise ideas and to train them to construct arguments more effectively. It can also develop thinking and reasoning skills.

Discuss the positive and negative effects of smartphones on society and the environment.

For thousands of years, people managed to live without smartphones. Yet in the 20 years since they were invented, our lives have been completely transformed. Although this transformation has been extremely positive on the whole, people are becoming far more conscious of the negative impact that smartphones have had.

Our dependence on smartphones affects the society we live in. These types of phone encourage individualism and selfishness. People in public spaces such as buses, cafes and restaurants are forced to listen to loud, private conversations. It has also become more difficult to interact with people in public as they continually take calls, respond to texts or check work emails.

Smartphones have become must-have accessories, and this means that young people feel that they always need to have the newest and most expensive models. This can lead young people, who do not earn very much and have to pay for rent and transport, into financial difficulties and possibly debt. There is also an environmental impact. Many smartphones only last for two years, which means that millions are thrown away every year.

Smartphones have had a negative impact on both society and the environment, but on balance I believe the effects on society are more significant. As people interact less and spend more time in their own worlds, there is a danger that we will gradually become more closed and selfish as a society. This can only be bad news for society.

The lesson described below is designed to help learners better understand how to write a discursive essay for a typical English language examination, such as the CAE or IELTS. To do this, the learners explore the reasons behind the writer's use of the present simple, the present progressive and the present perfect simple or continuous. However, it is important to note here that teachers should not focus exclusively on grammar when analysing this type of essay. Learners should also be helped to develop a broader understanding of cohesive devices, such as pronouns and determiners (*they, this, these*), cohesive noun phrases (*our dependence on … , this impact … , this uncertainty …*) or key technical terms (De Chazal, 2010). An example of this can be seen in the teaching tips below.

Lesson procedure

Lead-in: This can be done simply by displaying the essay title and asking learners to brainstorm the positive and negative effects that smartphones have had on people and the environment. In feedback, expand on student ideas and encourage them to justify their opinions.

Focus: The students read the essay and discuss whether they agree or disagree with the arguments presented. At this stage, it is a good idea to encourage the learners to present counter-arguments.

Uncovering reasons: Display the three model sentences below. Ask the students why the writer is using the following forms:

… our lives <u>have been completely transformed</u>.
<u>people are becoming</u> far more conscious of the negative impact …
Our dependence on smartphones <u>affects</u> the society we live in.

Think about

Before the lesson, try to formulate your own reasons for the examples above. How do they compare with the reasons below, formulated by a group of students at C1 level?

The writer is using the present perfect simple to connect the invention of phones (past) and the effect now.

The writer is using the present continuous to emphasise that the problem is ongoing now.

The writer is using the present simple to show a true fact according to the writer.

How can you use the reasons above to further clarify how the three forms are used within the text? It would be useful to look at other examples of discursive essays to see if these tenses are used in the same way.

Discussing reasons: Explore learner-generated reasons in feedback.

Teaching tips

As suggested above, it is also important to help learners develop a broader understanding of cohesion, and this can also be done by encouraging learners to explore reasons. As with grammar, the teacher displays examples from the text and asks the learners to discuss why the writer is using *this*.

> *Although <u>this transformation</u> has been extremely positive …*
> *… <u>this</u> means that young people feel they need to have the newest model.*
> *<u>This</u> can only be bad news for society.*

What reasons did you come up with? See the teacher's notes on page 184 for ideas.

Replication activity: There are a number of practice options available at this stage. For example, the learners can reconstruct the text using prompts or working from memory. Alternatively, the learners can write their own essay on the subject using the ideas generated in the lead-in. A more challenging option is to give the learners a new essay title.

Sharing work: The learners share their essays. In order to give the learners a purpose for reading each other's essays, ask them beforehand to consider whether they agree or disagree with the arguments presented by the writer.

Feedback loop: Display or distribute examples of interesting or incorrect language for analysis. Remember to use the frame *Why are you using …?* or *Why did you use …?* to encourage learners to focus on their use of specific forms.

Transposition activity: As one of the objectives of using discursive essays is to develop thinking skills and encouraging learners to construct arguments, a useful transposition task is to have a classroom debate. This involves learners taking the arguments from the essay and using them to argue either for or against a topic. In an exam class, this can also work as an effective break from developing exam strategies.

Lesson 9: School rules

A2 or early B1 level coursebooks regularly include activities that encourage students to practise using new structures by writing or completing lists of individual sentences. Though these types of activity are designed to help the learners produce the form of a structure accurately, they are often not particularly effective in helping them use new language for communicative purposes. However, there are some structures that actually suit this type of activity simply because the form is often found in lists. One such example is modal verbs of obligation.

The following text and lesson procedure is designed to enable learners at A2 or B1 level to understand and use a range of past modal verbs to talk about school rules in their countries. For slightly lower levels, this text can be simplified quite easily.

What were the worst rules in your school?

Following the news that a UK school has banned high fives and fist bumps for safety reasons, we wanted to hear about some of the rules in your schools. Were any of them as strange as this one?

Your comments

In my school we had to shine our shoes every evening or we were hit on the back of the hand with a ruler. I suppose they weren't so worried about us getting hurt. **Emma, Sheffield**

When I was in school, girls weren't allowed to wear make-up or earrings. **Yasmin, London**

We had to stand up whenever an adult entered the room. **Shahid, Herts**

In my boarding school we were allowed to wear our own clothes in the evenings and on the weekends. However, we weren't allowed to wear black for some reason. **Jake, Brecon**

I went to a mixed school but the boys had to sit on one side of the room and girls on the other. **Steve, Lancs**

We couldn't undo our top buttons anywhere in the school. That's why I never do my top button up today. **Danny, London**

In my school, all the boys had to have same haircut and your hair couldn't go past your eyebrows or collar. It was like being in the army. **Stephan, Belfast**

The teachers in my school were still allowed to use the cane. I remember being hit for really small things, like eating crisps in the hall and for having my socks rolled down. **Jo, Amsterdam**

In my school you didn't have to wear a uniform, but you couldn't wear trainers, jeans or caps either. In other words, nothing we actually wanted to wear. **Kate, Brighton**

I got sent home for wearing black make-up. I don't think there was a rule about this though. I just think the teacher didn't like me. **Aniya, Bucks**

Lesson procedure

Lead-in: Show pictures of old boarding schools or schools from 10–20 years ago. Encourage the students to discuss if they think these schools were stricter than they are today. It's also a good idea to show a picture of you at school. This can really get your learners' attention.

Focus: The students read the list of rules. In groups, they decide which ones are reasonable and which ones aren't. Alternatively, rank them from the strictest to the fairest. In feedback, it is good to discuss why a school might have those rules and if there are similar rules in the students' countries.

Teaching tips

As an alternative text you could search online for school rules from around the world. As a task, give the students a list of countries and a list of rules. Ask them to match the rules with the countries.

Uncovering reasons: Display the model sentences below. Ask the students why the writers are using the following forms.

We <u>had to shine</u> our shoes every evening or we were
hit on the back of the hand with a ruler.
<u>Girls weren't allowed to wear make-up or earrings</u>.
We <u>couldn't undo</u> our top buttons anywhere in the school.
We <u>were allowed to wear</u> our own clothes on the weekend.
In my school <u>we didn't have to wear</u> a uniform.

Think about

Before the lesson, try to formulate your own reasons for the examples above. How do they compare with the reasons below, formulated by a group of students at A2/B1 level?

They got a punishment if they <u>didn't</u> do it. (had to)

They got a punishment if they <u>did</u> it. (couldn't/weren't allowed to)

It's ok so there is no punishment. They choose to do it or they don't choose. (could/didn't have to)

Discussing reasons: Explore learner-generated reasons in feedback.

Replication activity: The learners create their own lists of rules. In a multilingual class, this is an excellent way of helping the students to learn more about their classmates and other cultures. To create more opportunities for discussion, some can be true and some can be false.

Sharing work: The learners share their rules, perhaps by reading them out to the whole class or displaying them around the classroom. At the end, the students can decide which school was the strictest and which one was the most liberal.

Feedback loop: Display or distribute examples of interesting or incorrect language for analysis. Remember to use the frame *Why are you using ….?* or *Why did you use …?* to encourage learners to focus on their use of specific forms.

Teaching tips

As a follow-up to this lesson, ask the class to create rules for your classroom. These are often known as classroom contracts. As well as encouraging learners to communicate and brainstorm ideas, classroom contracts enable you to set some ground rules without having to lay down the law. In fact, they enable the students to set some rules for you! Once the students have completed their lists, you can display them in the classroom.

This activity also enables you to explore how modals of obligation are used in the present (eg. *we have to come to class on time, we aren't allowed to text in class*). You can then formulate reasons for these too.

Lesson 10: Cheese rolling and wife carrying

In this lesson, learners read descriptions of two unusual festivals held in the UK every year. This is a lovely way to help students learn a little more about British culture and traditions. However, you may want to use texts that relate to your students' culture or to choose traditions from around the world.

Text A: Cheese rolling at Cooper's Hill	Text B: The wife carrying race in Dorset
Dating back to the 1880s, cheese rolling is an annual race held on the Spring Bank Holiday at Cooper's Hill near Gloucester in England.	The practice of wife carrying is said by some to date back to 793, when Viking raiders attacked the isle of Lindisfarne on the northeast coast, destroying the monastery and carrying off the unwilling local women.

It is traditionally for residents of the nearby village of Brockworth, but today people from all over the world come and take part. In fact, a 39-year-old Japanese man and a 27-year-old man from the USA each won one of the four races in 2013.

At the beginning of the race, competitors stand at the top of the hill. A 9 lb ball of Double Gloucester cheese is then rolled down the hill and the competitors start racing after it. However, nobody ever catches the cheese, which can reach speeds of up to 70 mph (112 km/h) and knock over spectators standing in its way. Instead, the winner is the first person to reach the bottom.

Because of the steepness of the hill and the uneven surface, the event usually sees a number of injuries. The most occurred in 1997 when 33 people were hurt, with injuries ranging from splinters to broken bones.

In 2008, the 'tradition' was revived in the form of a race now held annually in the village of Nower, Dorking. In the race, men and women must carry a 'wife' along a hilly 380-m course. Along the way, they need to tackle obstacles such as hay bales and hurdles and a splash zone, where locals throw buckets of cold water over the competitors. There are also time penalties for entrants who drop their 'wife'. The winners receive £100 and a barrel of local beer and gain entry into the world championships in Finland. The losers receive a ceremonial tin of dog food.

Competitors do not need to be married to their 'wives', but they need to be over 17 and must weigh at least 50 kg. Those that don't must make up the difference by carrying a rucksack filled with baked bean tins.

Text A: Cheese rolling at Cooper's Hill	Text B: The wife carrying race in Dorset
However, every year the event becomes more and more popular and it now attracts several thousand spectators.	Up to 50 couples can take part each year, and recent winners have come from South Africa, the USA and Italy. The event is now extremely popular, and was voted Britain's best adventure race in 2011.

Lesson procedure

Lead-in: Show pictures of the two events. The students try to guess what is happening in each picture.

Focus:

■ In pairs or small groups, the students write their own questions based on what they want to know about the texts. The questions are then displayed for the whole class.

■ Split the students into two groups. One group reads Text A (Cheese rolling) and the other reads Text B (Wife carrying). The students answer the questions displayed on the board.

■ Students then pair up with someone from the other group and tell them about their event. In pairs, the students decide which event they would like to attend or take part in and why.

Teaching tips

Jigsaw reading: This is a useful activity for students, as by giving the learners different texts to read, they are required to exchange information in order to achieve the task. Jigsaw reading also gives learners the opportunity to take part in a genuine communicative activity, as in real life we often tell people about something we have read in the news or online. This is why the activity often works well with newspaper articles or texts chosen by the students themselves.

Uncovering reasons: Display the three model sentences below. Ask the students why the writers are using the present simple

People from all over the world <u>come and take part</u>.
At the beginning of the race, competitors <u>stand</u> at the top of the hill.
The winners <u>receive</u> £100 and a barrel of local beer.

Think about

Before the lesson, try to formulate your own reasons for the examples above. How do they compare with the reasons below, formulated by a group of students at B1 level?

The writer is using the present simple because every year is the same.

The writer is using present simple because it is a tradition. It is the same every year.

Note also how each example sentence contains a general subject: *people*, *competitors* and *the winners*. It would be useful to draw learners' attention to the use of these general nouns as they may wish to include them in the replication task that follows.

Discussing reasons: Explore learner-generated reasons in feedback.

Replication task: The learners write a description of a festival, tradition or event in their country or one they have attended. If you have time, the students can research their festivals online, though it is important to ensure that they do not just copy and paste what they read into their texts.

Sharing work: The learners share their traditions, perhaps by displaying them around the classroom, working in small groups or doing mini presentations. The learners then discuss which events they would like to attend or take part in. You can also find videos of each event online.

Feedback loop: Display or distribute examples of interesting or incorrect language for analysis. Remember to use the frame *Why are you using …?* or *Why did you use …?* to encourage learners to focus on their use of specific forms.

Teaching tips

As a **transposition task**, the students could make brochures or posters advertising one of the events described in the text.

Lesson 11: Student dilemmas

By doing replication tasks in the classroom, L2 learners create a lot of texts and these can become a valuable resource for other students. As well as cutting down on work, there are a number of benefits of using learner-generated content in classes. First, it is more likely that students will be able to relate to the content of a text if they know it has been written by one of their peers or by someone in the same position as them. Learner-generated texts can also be extremely motivating, as they show learners what they are capable of achieving. If another student can do it, so can they. For teachers without access to much material or for those who rely on coursebooks, learner-generated texts can provide a rich source of relevant and engaging material that is appropriate to the level of the class. In addition, the source never runs out.

In this lesson, the learners read dilemmas written by other students studying at their school. These texts have already been corrected by a teacher, but like the authentic text they replicate, they include examples of the modal verbs *will* and *would* used in *if* clauses. This can lead students to an interesting discovery about these two verbs and the use of conditional forms.

Your questions answered

It is hard to decide where I want to go to university. If I stay in Taiwan, I'll be able to stay with my family. I can also learn a lot from my father and follow in his footsteps. But if I go to the USA, it would be much more cosmopolitan and I would learn a lot from standing on my own two feet. The problem is that my parents want me to stay in Taiwan and take over the family business. They think that family is the most important thing and that I should put family first. **Jay, Taiwan**

I have to decide whether to change my son's school or not. Right now he's going to an international school, but people say that as I'm living here, he should go to a British school. I think a British school would give him a broader education, but if he stays where he is, he won't have to start another new school. **Yoshimi, Japan**

My problem is I don't like getting up early and coming to school, but I don't like getting on packed trains in rush hour either. **Vieri, Italy**

Lesson procedure

Lead-in: Tell the students a dilemma or problem that you are having and ask for advice.

Focus: The students read the texts and discuss what Jay, Yoshimi and Vieri should do.

Uncovering reasons: Display the three model sentences below. Ask the students why the writers are using *will* and *would* in the *if* clauses.

If I stay in Taiwan, I'll be able to stay with my family.
If I go to the USA, it would be more cosmopolitan and I would learn a lot from standing on my own two feet.
… a British school would give him a broader education, but if he stays in the international school, he won't have to start another new school.

Think about

Before the lesson, try to formulate your own reasons for the examples above. How do they compare with the reasons below, formulated by a group of students at B2 level?

If + *present simple* + **will** *is the easy choice because the situation is already true now. There are no big changes.*

If + *present simple* + **would** *is less easy choice .†† There is more change.*

In coursebooks, *if* clauses tend to be neatly packaged into four conditionals. *Will* is found in the first conditional (*If* + present + *will* + infinitive), which describes things that could possibly happen. *Would* is used in the second conditional (*If* + past simple + *would* + infinitive) to express things that are unlikely, impossible or unreal. However, when we look at Jay's dilemma, we can see an example of *would* used with the present simple: *If I go to the USA, it would be more cosmopolitan and I would learn a lot from standing on my own two feet.* How is he able to do this?

It is because both choices are perceived as possible. He could choose to go to the USA or he could choose to stay in Taiwan. This is demonstrated through the use of the present simple in the *if* clause (*If I stay in Taiwan, If I go to the USA*).

The distinction comes in the second clause, where *will* and *would* are used. In the first example, Jay uses *will* (*I'll be able to stay with my family*) because this is something he already does, so the outcome of his future actions will be familiar. However, in the second sentence, the outcome will be unfamiliar (*it would be more cosmopolitan and I would learn a lot from standing on my own two feet*) and he will need to make adjustments. This suggests that going to the USA will be the more difficult choice. This is something that the students have recognised in the reasons above.

Discussing reasons: Explore learner-generated reasons in feedback.

Replication task: The learners write their own dilemmas. These can be serious, as Jay's and Yoshimi's are, or more humorous, like Vieri's.

Sharing work: The learners share their dilemmas with the rest of the class, perhaps by reading them out or displaying them around the room. As in the lead-in and reading task, the students give each other advice.

Feedback loop: Display or distribute examples of interesting or incorrect language for analysis. Remember to use the frame '*Why are you using …?*' or '*Why did you use …?*' to encourage learners to focus on their use of specific forms.

Teaching tips

As well as being interesting and engaging content for other classes, learner-generated texts can be used to help other students notice and correct common errors. This is especially useful if the texts have been written by learners who speak the same L1.

Lesson 12: The magic camera

This is the first of the more task-based lessons. This lesson was suggested to me a number of years ago and it is a wonderful way to get students to share stories and learn about each other. Over the years, I've heard some very funny anecdotes, such as the student who got stuck at the top of one of the pyramids, or the one who fell asleep on a phone box after their graduation.

I've heard some incredibly moving stories too. All you need is paper, pens and some memories.

Lesson procedure

Lead-in:

■ Before class, draw 1–3 'photographs' that depict events in your life that you would like to share with your students.

■ Tell the students that you are going to show them a 'photograph' of a memorable moment in your life. Once you have shown them the 'photo', the students can try to predict what happened or ask you questions about it. Alternatively, you can just begin the lesson by telling them the story.

■ Give the learners photo-sized cards, pencils or coloured pens and ask them to draw their own 'photos'. They can do any number up to three.

Task:

■ Once they have drawn their 'photos', prepare them for the communicative task by providing them with prompts for their story, for example, *Where were you when you took the photo? What were you doing there? What had you been doing earlier?* To do this, I like to get the students to close their eyes and visualise the story. As they do so, I read out questions as prompts.

Teaching tips

Using visualisation techniques: Moreillon (2007) claims that some of our most powerful memories are attached to sensory experiences, and that a smell or a taste can trigger a long-cherished memory. As you ask your students to visualise the events in their photos, ask them to think about how they felt, what else they could see or what they could hear. This may just prompt them to remember something else about their story.

■ The students perform the task. With a small group this can be done as a whole class activity. For larger classes, split the students into groups of four or five. Lay all the 'photos' out and ask the students to choose which one they want to hear about first. The student who drew the 'photo' talks about it and the rest of the group listen and ask questions. When they have finished talking, the speaker then chooses another student's 'photo'. Repeat until everyone has had a go.

■ Monitor carefully and listen to their ideas. After each student has had a turn, display some ideas on the board. If any examples are inaccurate or inappropriate, work with the class to reformulate them.

Uncovering reasons: Highlight examples of language that students produce during the task. Ask the learners why they are using any particular forms, for example:

We <u>*were driving back*</u> *to the exit of the national park.*
We <u>hadn't really seen</u> anything all day.
Suddenly this elephant just <u>appeared</u> and started smashing up a tree right in front of us.

Think about

Before the lesson, try to formulate your own reasons for forms you expect your students to use in the lesson. How do they compare with the reasons below, formulated by a group of students at B2 level?

Past continuous is the background to the story. It takes us to the beginning.

Past perfect takes us back if we need to go back. It tells us about the time before you take the photo. †

The past simple takes us forward in the story.

How can you use the reasons above to further clarify how the three forms are used? Consider how you might use a timeline to do this. For an example, see the teacher's notes on page 185.

Discussing reasons: Explore learner-generated reasons in feedback.

Replication task: The students can now repeat the task by talking about a different 'photo'.

Sharing work/feedback loop: As the students do this, you can make a note of interesting language or errors for each student. They can then take this away to study for homework.

Lesson 13: The ranking task

Sometimes all you need for an interesting task-based lesson is a list of words. This can be one you bring in, or you can generate one with the students at the start of the class.

In this lesson and the next (Lesson 14), you will see how a list of jobs can be used to set up a range of open-ended speaking tasks. These tasks can then be used to help students explore a range of language items, from modal verbs such as *should* and *can*, to ways of negotiating or agreeing and disagreeing.

teacher	builder
doctor	soldier
judge	refuse collector
nurse	engineer
politician	lawyer
police officer	farmer

Lesson procedure

Lead-in: If you want to keep it simple, the students can brainstorm different types of jobs or tell each other what jobs they do or would like to do. If you have more time, however, ask the students to brainstorm a list of the most important jobs in the world. Extend this stage by encouraging students to justify their ideas.

Task:

- Hand out or display the list of jobs. Students work individually to rank the jobs according to how much they earn, that is, they put them in order from the highest to the lowest pay.

- When they have finished, put students into pairs to compare their lists. They then have to work together to compile a new list. To do this, they have to agree on the order.

- In feedback, display the final list as agreed by the groups and discuss any differences. Then tell the students they are going to do the task again. However, this time they have to decide which jobs *should* be paid the most. Tell the students that they have to justify their opinions.

- Students repeat the task.

- Monitor carefully and listen to their ideas. When the students have finished speaking, display some ideas on the board, as seen below. If any examples are inaccurate or inappropriate, work with the class to reformulate them.

Teaching tips

One way of doing this task is to set up a **pyramid discussion**. This is a type of speaking activity in which learners perform the same task in progressively larger groups. In this lesson, for example, the learners work alone to put the jobs in order. When they have finished, they are paired with another student in order to do the same task. However, in this stage, each pair needs to reach an agreement. Once this is done, they can then join another group and the process starts again.

As well as generating a lot of discussion, pyramid discussions are very useful for practising functional language, such as negotiating, agreeing and disagreeing and putting forward arguments. Because the students start off by working individually, it also gives quieter, less confident students time to prepare for the communicative work that follows. This ensures that everyone is more likely to get a turn.

Uncovering reasons: Highlight examples of language that students produced during the task. Ask the learners why they are using any particular forms, for example:

We think lawyers or judges probably <u>earn</u> the most.
We think judges <u>get</u> the most money.
Doctors and nurses <u>should</u> be higher because everyone needs them.
We think farmers <u>should</u> earn the most because they feed us.

Think about

Before the lesson, try to formulate your own reasons for forms you expect your students to use in the lesson. How do they compare with the reasons below, formulated by a group of students at A2/B1 level?

The first two is only fact. It's not opinion. We don't say if this is right or wrong. †

The second it's our ideas and opinion. We think this is the right way. †

Discussing reasons: Explore learner-generated reasons in feedback.

Replication activity: A simple replication activity is for students to repeat the task in new groups. However, there is a danger that this can be a bit repetitive, so it is important that the teacher makes it clear that this is to give the students the opportunity to redo the task and use the target language more effectively or consciously. Alternatively, you could hand out a new list of jobs (model, footballer, actor, lawyer, chef etc) to give the lesson some variety.

Sharing work/feedback loop: Display or distribute examples of interesting or incorrect language for analysis. Remember to use the frame *Why are you using ...?* or *Why did you use ...?* to encourage learners to focus on their use of specific forms.

Teaching tips

As suggested earlier, in a task-based lesson like this one, the teacher does not need to focus solely on grammatical structures in feedback. They can instead explore and reformulate students' use of functional language, such as ways of agreeing or disagreeing. It is also a good idea to explore speaking strategies such as turn-taking, interrupting or asking for clarification.

Lesson 14: The balloon debate

A list of jobs is all you need for a lively and enjoyable speaking task known as a balloon debate.

Balloon debates are so-called because the typical example is of a hot-air balloon which is rapidly losing height because it is carrying too much weight. To prevent the balloon from crashing, it is necessary to throw some of the passengers overboard. Therefore, a decision needs to be made.

Balloon debates are often used on business courses or as team-building exercises. This is due to the fact that they test people's decision-making skills and their ability to present reasonable arguments, both of which are considered to be vital management skills. On a training course, participants usually have about 30 minutes to study the problem and to prepare their arguments. It is of course up to you how much time you give your learners. For language students, this task can be used to help students explore a range of language items such as *should* and *can*, ways of negotiating or agreeing and disagreeing.

teacher	carpenter
doctor	soldier
judge	engineer
nurse	fisherman
mechanic	cook
police officer	farmer
electrician	vet

This lesson can be done in the traditional way where the students are given the list and they have to decide which five to seven jobs should be thrown overboard. In the lesson below, however, the students are given a job each. They therefore have to prepare their arguments for staying on the balloon before they present (or plead) their case to the rest of the class. The lesson finishes with a vote.

Teaching tips

I like to set the scene by telling the students that the world has been overrun by zombies and that they are in a balloon on their way to the safety of a desert island. It can help if you draw pictures as you tell the story.

It is also good to embellish the scenario and, by doing so, add an element of critical thinking to the task. Therefore, as you set the scene, feed in information that is relevant to the task. For example:

- The sea around the island is rich in fish but shark-infested.
- The island is baking hot during the day but cold at night.
- There is a large forest in the centre of the island.
- It is completely uninhabited by humans, although there are wild animals.

By adding such detail, the learners are forced to use factual information to help them prepare their arguments and justify why they should stay on the balloon. They can also use this information to prepare arguments for why other passengers should lose their place.

Lesson procedure

Lead-in: Engage the learners in the topic and set up the balloon debate.

Task:

- Give each student one of the jobs. If you have a large class, students can be split into different groups so that there are two or three debates happening at the same time. Alternatively, students can work in pairs to prepare their arguments and plead their case. As students prepare, monitor carefully, helping out with useful lexis and ideas.

- Students present their arguments and debate each other's ideas. At the end, the students vote on who should be thrown out of the balloon.

- Monitor carefully and listen to their ideas. When the students have finished speaking, discuss ideas in open-class and display examples of learner language on the board. If any examples are inaccurate or inappropriate, work with the class to reformulate them.

Uncovering reasons: Highlight examples of language that students produced during the task. Ask the learners why they are using any particular forms, for example:

I <u>should stay</u> on the balloon because I am the only one who <u>can</u> build us houses.
<u>If people are sick the doctor can help</u>. We don't need two doctors.
A judge <u>can't do anything</u> and they're always old!

Think about

Before the lesson, try to formulate your own reasons for forms you expect your students to use in the lesson. How do they compare with the reasons below, formulated by a group of students at A2/B1 level?

Should is my opinion and idea. It shows a good idea to choose me. ††

Can is my ability.

If shows future possibility for why keep the doctor. People will be sick. ††

Can't shows no good ability for the judge is why we don't keep him. ††

Discussing reasons: Explore learner-generated reasons in feedback.

Transposition task: As a follow-up task or a homework activity, students can write a letter or make a speech explaining why they should not be thrown out of the balloon. This then provides further communicative practice and gives the opportunity for students to consciously use the forms they have noticed in the feedback.

Sharing work/feedback loop: Display or distribute examples of interesting or incorrect language for analysis. Remember to use the frame *Why are you using ….?* or *Why did you use …?* to encourage learners to focus on their use of specific forms. If the transposition task was done for homework, ask the same questions either in the margins or below the student's work.

Teaching tips

As suggested in this lesson, the teacher does not need to focus solely on grammatical structures in feedback. For higher level students, you can focus on the ways that students present, justify and respond to ideas and arguments. This is especially useful for students who are intending to go to university in an English-speaking country or for those who have to write discursive essays.

Lesson 15: The go-between

This is an enjoyable communicative task, inspired by an activity created by Jill Hadfield (1990) in which students play the role of flatmates who have stopped speaking to one another. As well as leading to some lively discussions, the task helps students explore how reported speech is used to pass on messages.

The task also highlights an issue with a common pedagogic grammar rule and the type of controlled practice exercises frequently used in coursebooks and tests. However, by exploring reasons and using communicative tasks, this issue can be avoided.

Student A

You are annoyed with your flatmate and have stopped talking to him/her. You wish (s)he would:

- do a fair share of the washing up
- stop leaving dirty dishes around the flat
- stop playing music so loudly when you are trying to study.

Tell the go-between what you want but remember you are <u>not</u> talking to your flatmate.

Student B

You are annoyed with your flatmate and have stopped talking to him/her. You wish (s)he would:

- spend less time in the shower and stop using all the hot water
- stop tidying away your books, notebooks and laptop

- ■ stop clattering around in the kitchen early in the morning.

Tell the go-between what you want but remember you are <u>not</u> talking to your flatmate.

Student C

You share a house with two flatmates. However, they have stopped talking to each other.

You want to fix the problem, so you need to carry messages from one flatmate to the other. You must report exactly what they say.

Continue delivering messages until the problems are solved.

Lesson procedure

Lead-in. Students brainstorm examples of what makes a bad flatmate. The teacher displays ideas on the board.

Task:

- ■ Put the students into groups of three. One is flatmate A, one is flatmate B and the other student is the go-between. Hand out the role cards. Give the students time to prepare for the role play, helping with any unknown words or phrases.

- ■ Students perform the task. At the end, the students should have reached some kind of agreement.

- ■ Monitor carefully and listen to their ideas. When the students have finished speaking, discuss ideas in open-class and display examples of learner language on the board. If any examples are inaccurate or inappropriate, work with the class to reformulate them.

Uncovering reasons: Use examples of learner language from the task to highlight the use of present verb forms in reported speech. Ask the learners why they were using or could have used the following forms:

He said <u>you take</u> too long in the shower and <u>he can't use</u> it.
He said <u>he wants</u> you to do the washing up more.
He said that <u>if you wash up</u> more, <u>he will stop tidying</u> up your things.

Think about

Before the lesson, try to formulate your own reasons for the use of present simple in the examples of reported speech above. How do they compare with the reasons below, formulated by a group of students at B1 level?

He said it in the past but the problem is still now.
He asked in the past but he wants the change to happen now.

In reported speech, it is possible to change the form of the verb in the **reported** clause by moving it **back** one tense. For example, the present simple can become the past simple, as in '*He said he <u>wanted</u> you to do the washing up more*'. This is known as backshift.

Unfortunately, it is common to see coursebooks state that after *said*, the verb in the reported clause has to backshift. However, this is one of those occasions when the rule is not strictly true. It is also quite unhelpful. To compound matters, traditional controlled practice exercises and tests frequently ask learners to transform sentences from direct speech into reported speech by backshifting the verb, often without guidance or context (Parrott, 2010). This will only lead to confusion and questions when students inevitably encounter examples of reported speech in authentic texts and genuine communicative situations.

In this role play, there is little need to change present forms into past forms. This is because the go-between is technically passing on present requests. However, it would be possible to use backshift on some occasions, as can be seen below.

He said he wants you to do the washing-up more.
He said he wanted you to do the washing-up more.

In the next pair of examples however, backshifting the verb would actually cause confusion. The key is, therefore, to bypass the rule and explore the reason instead.

He said you take too long in the shower. (You always do this; it's a habit.)
He said you took too long in the shower. (This could only have happened on one occasion.)

Discussing reasons: Explore learner-generated reasons in feedback.

Replication task: Mix the students up so there are new go-betweens in each group. The students perform the task again, perhaps with different scenarios (eg. couples, colleagues).

Sharing work/feedback loop: Display or distribute examples of interesting or incorrect language for analysis. Remember to use the frame *Why are you using ...?* or *Why did you use ...?* to encourage learners to focus on their use of specific forms.

Teaching tips

As a **transposition task**, the students could write an email from one flatmate to another. This would enable the students to explore how to be tactful and use polite expressions when complaining about something and making requests.

Lesson 16: The job interview

A list of questions can form the basis for an interesting task-based lesson.

In the following procedure, the learners work with a list of questions or prompts commonly asked in job interviews. Once they have discussed the purpose of the questions and how they can be successfully answered, the students then role-play the interview.

What are your strengths and weaknesses?
What would your colleagues say are your best qualities?
Why do you want to work here?
Why did you leave your last job?
Where do you see yourself in five years' time?
Tell us about a difficult situation you faced and how you dealt with it.
What has been your greatest achievement?
How do you manage your time?
If you were an animal, what animal would you be?
Why should we hire you?

In this lesson, the way that the learners explore reasons is different. This is because rather than explore the use of specific forms directly, the students instead formulate the reasons for the questions. This can help learners uncover an interesting and common use of the second conditional.

Lesson procedure

Lead-in:

- If the students have experience of job interviews, you can start the lesson by asking them to share stories. Alternatively, display an advertisement for a job you believe your learners would be interested in. The students then brainstorm the qualities and skills needed to do the job and discuss what they need to do before attending an interview.

- Hand out the list of questions. In order to focus on the role of the participants in the interview, discuss why the interviewer would ask each question and what answers they are expecting.

Teaching tips

Job interview questions are not significantly different around the world. However, the way that they should be answered can differ enormously. In your own country or culture, it is easier to know what to expect and how to behave in the interview. Yet in another country, a job interview can be an extremely challenging experience. It is therefore very useful to spend time exploring the purpose of questions and interview tasks and looking at how they can be answered successfully in different contexts and countries.

Uncovering reasons: Display the example questions below. Ask why the interviewer is asking these questions and what answers they might expect.

What are your strengths and weaknesses?
What has been your greatest achievement?
Where do you see yourself in five years' time?
If you were an animal, what animal would you be?

Think about

Before the lesson, try to formulate your own reasons for why an interviewer would ask these questions. How do they compare with the reasons below, formulated by a group of students at B2 level?

They want to know your character.

They want to know about your experience.

They want to know your motivation/They want to see if you are ambitious.

They want to surprise you and see an interesting answer. †

Note that for the second conditional (*If you were an animal, what animal would you be?*) the purpose of the question is to see if the interviewee can think on their feet and be creative. This is very different from the typical rule for the second conditional found in coursebooks and grammars, that is, that 'the Second Conditional is used to talk about "impossible" or "unreal" situations'. This rule is true, but by exploring reasons, we are able to demonstrate to students *why* a speaker might use the form in a genuine conversation and what they expect from the answer. This would be an interesting area to explore in feedback.

Discussing reasons: Explore learner-generated reasons in feedback.

Task: When students are ready, put them into pairs to role-play the interviews. Listen and note down examples of questions that were answered successfully and unsuccessfully.

Sharing work: This stage is optional. However, if the students need to attend job interviews, this part of the lesson can be recorded. The students can then listen to themselves and consider how well they answered each question.

Feedback loop: Display or distribute examples of interesting or incorrect language for analysis. Remember to use the frame *Why are you using …?* or *Why did you use …?* to encourage learners to focus on their use of specific forms.

Lesson 17: What happened?

A number of years ago, some trainee teachers on a course at my school were enthusing about a lesson they had just observed. In the lesson, the teacher walked into the classroom with paint on her shoes and at the bottom of her trousers. The students then had to guess what had happened to her. Once this was done, she told them the story (a man had spilt paint on her on the bus).

What had most fascinated the trainees was the amount of language that was generated by this situation. They were also surprised at the complexity of some of the language explored in the lesson considering the relatively low level of the class.

The following procedure demonstrates how a lesson can be based simply on the learners' curiosity. It also shows how simple, communicative tasks can be used at lower levels to generate a lot of new language. Because students know what they want to say, this subsequently enables the teacher to explore words, phrases and grammatical forms that might be considered too complex for the level and unlikely to be included in a low level coursebook.

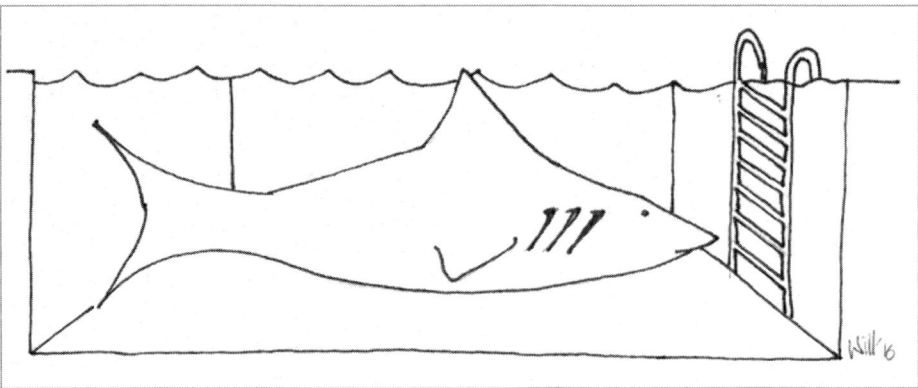

Lesson procedure

Lead-in: Find some unusual photographs online and bring them into class. In this lesson, I used a photograph of a shark in a swimming pool, a car on a roof and a bride and her bridesmaids on a bus. The students then have to guess what has happened.

Task:

- Students perform the task. To extend the task, give them a good amount of time to speculate or give them a set number of predictions. You can also award prizes for the most inventive idea.

- Monitor carefully and listen to their ideas. When the students have finished speaking, discuss ideas in open-class and display examples of learner language on the board. If any examples are inaccurate or inappropriate, work with the class to reformulate them.

Uncovering reasons: Use examples of learner language from the task to highlight the use of speculative language. Ask the learners why they are using any particular forms, for example:

> *<u>Maybe</u> the hotel <u>owns</u> the shark. It's a friendly shark.*
> *It <u>could have fallen from a plane</u>.*
> *<u>Maybe</u> their limousine <u>broke down</u>.*

Think about

Before the lesson, try to formulate your own reasons for the use of speculative language. How do they compare with the reasons below, formulated by a group of students at A2/B1 level?

It's possible now but we don't know.

It's the past but we don't know what happen. ††

We guess the past but we don't know exactly the past. †

It might be thought that learners at A2/B1 would not be able to cope with a structure such as *might/could + have +* past participle. For this reason, past modals of deduction are often first introduced in intermediate coursebooks. However, as the reasons above demonstrate, learners at lower levels are more than capable of understanding this supposedly complex structure. The reason is because the students know what they want to say. The teacher then helps them to say it more accurately by reformulating their ideas and providing a correct model. In this sense, therefore, the students provide the meaning and the teacher supplies the form (Wilberg, 2010).

Teaching tips

Drilling: Due to its association with behaviourist theories, which suggested that learning another language was simply a matter of forming correct habits through repetition, drilling was seen as an important aspect of the audio-lingual approach. Because we now know that languages are not learned through this technique alone, language drills have fallen out of favour in more communicative approaches.

However, drilling remains a useful classroom technique, especially when it is used to reinforce meaning or to demonstrate the function of a sentence. Take the following examples from this lesson:

It _could_ have fallen from a plane.

Maybe their limousine broke down.

It _must_ have fallen from a plane

To reinforce the fact that the speaker is speculating, the teacher can focus on aspects of pronunciation that indicate this. For example, they can highlight the use of questioning intonation. In addition, they can demonstrate how the stressed words _could_ and _maybe_ might be stretched out by the speaker. If the modals _must_ or _can't_ were used, this would not happen, as the speaker is much more certain. Short classroom drills would demonstrate this, thereby reinforcing the meaning.

Discussing reasons: Explore learner-generated reasons in feedback.

Transposition task: Put the students into pairs or small groups. The students then write a short newspaper article reporting what happened in one of the photographs. Alternatively, this could be done as a spoken new report. This is a very effective transposition task, as it enables the students to explore the difference between the speculative language in the first task (maybe their limousine broke down) with the factual language used in a report (On the way to the wedding, their limousine broke down).

Sharing work/feedback loop: Display or distribute examples of interesting or incorrect language for analysis. Remember to use the frame _Why are you using …?_ or _Why did you use …?_ to encourage learners to focus on their use of specific forms.

Lesson 18: Battersea Power Station

What would you do with the power station?

It is important to note that there is a lot of scope for adapting this lesson. For example, the teacher can choose any iconic building or one that is relevant to a particular group of learners. The pre-task or planning stage can include a recording of people doing the task. This could be two teachers or students from a higher level class. This gives the learners ideas for the task and provides a clear model of what they need to do. This stage can also be used to provide examples of language that the students can use when they perform the tasks.

However, the tasks described below are examples of free or unfocused tasks. This means that the learners are not provided with models of language and are free to use whatever language they have available in order to complete the task. In terms of analysing reasons, the language models the teacher uses will come from the students.

Working with emerging language in this way may sound daunting. However, due to the nature of the tasks, it is possible to predict the type of grammatical items that are likely to occur. In this particular sequence of lessons, therefore, we will see how learners formulate reasons for their own uses of *would, could* and *should* along with *will* and *going to*.

Lesson procedure Part 1

Lead-in:

- Display a picture of the building and find out what students know or can guess about it. You could also make a recording of someone talking about the building, describing some history, what they like about it and why it is iconic.

- Tell the students that the government or local council has decided that the building is going to be turned into luxury flats. Discuss why people might be angry or disappointed by this decision.

Task:

- Put the students into pairs or small groups. They have to think of five alternative uses for the building. The only criterion is that it must remain open to the public.

- Monitor carefully and listen to their ideas. When the students have finished speaking, discuss ideas in open-class and display examples of learner language on the board. If any examples are inaccurate or inappropriate, work with the class to reformulate them.

Uncovering reasons: Highlight examples of language that students produced during the task. Ask the learners why they are using any particular forms, for example:

> It _would be good_ if they turned it into a museum.
> It _could be_ a concert hall or music venue.
> It _could be_ a museum of alternative culture.
> _We would turn_ it into an art gallery.

Think about

Before the lesson, try to formulate your own reasons for the examples above. How do they compare with the reasons below, formulated by a group of students at B1 level?

It _would be good if_ … means it's a nice idea but it won't happen because of money.

Would is our imagination. It's a wish or a hope we can't do. †

Could is for ideas and recommendations. It's not like a hope or a wish.

How can you use the reasons above to help learners better understand the difference between *would* and *could*. Consider also how the phrase *It would be good if ...* suggests that someone or something is blocking the outcome the speaker desires.

Discussing reasons: Explore the learner-generated reasons in feedback.

Lesson procedure Part 2

Lead-in:

■ Display or hand out a list of potential uses for the power station.

a museum	an art gallery	a shopping centre
a sports stadium	a park	a music venue
an open-air cinema	an arts centre	a skate-park

Task:

■ Put the students into new groups. The students now have to work together to choose the best idea. To ensure there is some discussion and negotiation, different students in the group could be given different options from the list. They then have to persuade their partners that their idea is the best one.

■ Give students time to prepare ideas and arguments.

■ Students perform the task. When all the students have presented their ideas, give the groups time to choose the best option. They will therefore need to use their negotiation skills to decide on which idea they will present.

■ Monitor carefully and listen to their ideas. When the students have finished speaking, discuss ideas in open-class and display examples of learner language on the board. If any examples are inaccurate or inappropriate, work with the class to reformulate them.

Uncovering reasons: Highlight examples of language that students produced during the task. Ask the learners why they were using *should* in their discussions, as in the following examples.

I think <u>we should make</u> a park as there isn't a good park on the river.
I <u>don't think we should build</u> another art gallery by the river.

Think about

Before the lesson, try to formulate your own reasons for the examples above. How do they compare with the reasons below, formulated by a group of students at B1 level? How successful have the learners been in describing why they were using *should* in the activity?

We are using should because we believe in our idea. We want to persuade the other students to choose our idea.

Note that in a task such as this, the teacher should not limit the input by focusing on one or two grammatical items. In fact, the task could quite easily be performed without the use of *should*. Therefore it is important to remember that tasks are an extremely effective way of introducing learners to a range of functional expressions and lexical phrases. The teacher can also look at speaking skills such as taking or holding a turn.

To help learners reflect on the reasons behind the use of lexical phrases in feedback, the teacher can simply ask *Why did we use the following phrases?*

■ *We think a music venue <u>would</u> be really popular.*
■ *<u>If we create</u> a music venue, <u>It'll promote</u> the arts and bring tourists to this part of London.*
■ *<u>Yes, but</u> that's not going to bring in any money.*
■ *<u>Sorry, can I finish?</u>*

See the teacher's notes on page 187 for suggested answers.

Lesson procedure Part 3

Lead-in: Tell the students that they are now going to present their ideas to the rest of the group.

Teaching tips

At this stage there are a number of options available to the teacher. They can choose to let students go straight into their presentations or they can give them time to prepare. If there is time or if the lesson can run over into a second day, the students can create PowerPoint slides, visuals or posters. The teacher can also provide the students with useful language models. Regardless of the level of support the students receive, encouraging them to perform tasks publicly means that they are more likely to think about the quality of their language use as they know it will be viewed by the whole class (Batstone, 2007).

Task:

- The students present their ideas to the rest of the class.

- After all the students have presented their ideas, the class votes for the best one.

- Monitor carefully and listen to their ideas. When the students have finished speaking, discuss ideas in open-class and display examples of learner language on the board. If any examples are inaccurate or inappropriate, work with the class to reformulate them.

Uncovering reasons: Highlight examples of language that students produced during the task. Ask the learners to formulate reasons for any interesting and useful language used in the presentation. This is likely to include examples of *will* (used to make promises and pledges, as seen in Lesson 6) and *going to* (to describe plans and intentions). The present simple with verbs such as *intend to* or *plan to* can also be used:

> We <u>will</u> turn Battersea Power station into a park and music venue.
> We are <u>going to</u> create a large park with space for galleries and stalls.
> We <u>intend to</u> build a museum.

Think about

Before the lesson, try to formulate your own reasons for the examples above. How do they compare with the reasons below, formulated by a group of students at B1 level? How successful have the learners been in describing why they were using *will* and *going to* in the activity?

We are using will and going to because this is our plan. We need to show our plan in a presentation.

Feedback loop: At the end of the lesson, display or distribute examples of interesting or incorrect language used in the three tasks for analysis.

Remember to use the frame *Why are you using …?* or *Why did you use …?* to encourage learners to focus on their use of specific forms.

Teaching tips

Why might it be more effective to explore language use after learners complete the task rather than before?

A common feature of a task-based lesson is a reflection stage, in which the learners consider the quality of the language they have used during the communicative stages. This can be done to explore how certain forms are used or to encourage the learners to notice gaps and think about possible improvements. A post-task reflection stage can also be used to uncover reasons, and in this lesson procedure, the following prompts can help learners formulate reasons for the use of *would, could, should* and *going to/ will,* and to consider the fact that different task types require different forms. In order to do this, use the following prompts:

- Why did we use *would* and *could* in Part 1?
- Why did we use *should* in Part 2?
- Why did we use *going to* and *will* in our presentations (Part 3)?

This is an effective way to close the lesson and to demonstrate to students what they have learnt.

2. Creating your own resources

Although it is possible to use the materials in the previous section with a number of different classes and types of learners, it would be unrealistic to claim that they could be appropriate for every cultural and educational context. However, the techniques and procedures used in the lessons have a broad application and can easily be adopted by teachers who wish to design their own materials and lessons. This part of Section 2 offers guidance and suggestions on how this can be done.

It includes:

- a suggested criteria for choosing texts and topics
- tips on how to design lead-ins
- suggestions on how to help learners engage meaningfully with texts
- templates for designing tasks
- a lesson planning task.

A criteria for choosing texts

Materials that have an impact with a class in Algeria might not necessarily achieve the same impact with a different group of learners in the UK. For this reason, it is important that teachers think carefully about the appropriacy of the materials they use with their students. Naturally, many teachers are able to rely on their experience and intuition when choosing or designing suitable materials. However, it is also useful to work from a framework or a set of criteria that outline important areas to consider. This is especially helpful for newer teachers or for those designing materials for the first time. Consider the following when choosing or designing materials.

1. **Relevance**

Texts and topics should be relevant to the learners' lives and interests. For example, a lot of the material in this publication was originally designed for adult learners living and studying in the UK, and this is reflected in the content of many of the texts. However, where a review of a London restaurant might be interesting and relevant for learners studying in the UK, the topic does not generally reflect the realities or experiences of many learners of English. This can potentially make both the topic and the text unengaging and demotivating, which in turn can make it harder for learners to respond to the material. The choice of text and topic is therefore extremely important.

2. **Culture**

It is a good idea for teachers to choose texts that represent their students' culture. Because many commercially produced coursebooks have been designed to appeal to as broad a range of learners as possible, it is naturally difficult for writers to include culturally specific texts or topics. This can mean that where the coursebook substitutes as a syllabus, learners can go through an entire English learning programme without ever working with materials that discuss or represent their culture. This might not only be demotivating but can also give learners a negative view of the language they are learning. It is important that, where possible, teachers try to include culturally specific material in their lessons and courses. Along with relevant topics, courses could include materials and texts that contain examples of the students' L1 or local or cultural references. The teacher can also try to find texts that were created by members of the students' culture or speakers of their language. As well as being motivating for learners, this type of material provides them with a model of what can be achieved. For multicultural or multilingual classes, using culturally diverse texts has the added benefit of potentially exposing learners to more varieties of English or to texts that reflect how English is used as a lingua franca by many speakers whose first language is not english.

3. **Learner need**

Texts should relate to the needs of the learners. For example, where a discursive essay is useful for students studying for an exam or for those that wish to attend an English-speaking university, it may not be as useful for students who want to learn English for work purposes or those that need it in order to integrate into an English-speaking community. The right level of materials is also important. If a text is too simplistic or overly challenging, learners can quickly become disengaged from the content. Learner need is something that teachers must be attuned to before they choose or create materials.

4. **Interest**

Above all else, texts should be interesting and engaging and capable of creating some kind of impact (Tomlinson, 2011). This ensures that learners are more likely to respond to the content of the materials, leading to greater engagement in the language work that follows. It is clearly a good idea to look for content that will arouse curiosity, stimulate debate, evoke feelings or encourage learners to think more deeply about a topic or situation. It is also good to look for texts about unusual topics or novel ideas, or to encourage students to bring in texts that they wish to discuss.

Once teachers have chosen their materials, they need to consider how they will engage learners in texts and how they will encourage them to read or listen to the content. This will be looked at in the next two subsections.

Designing lead-ins

As seen in the teaching resources, in order to prepare the learners for processing texts for meaning and form, it is common to begin the lesson with a lead-in. This is designed firstly to engage the learners in the content of the text and the topic of the lesson. However, a good lead-in can also help to activate our learners' schema, or their pre-existing knowledge of the topic (Cook, 1989). This can help the students to predict what the text might be about and enable them to share ideas and experiences relating to the topic or the participants in the text (Dörnyei, 2009). A prediction task can also be used to sensitise learners to difficult aspects of the text, such as organisation, accents, features of connected speech or typical genre features. This is thought to make the process of reading or listening in a second language that little bit easier.

A number of different activities can be used in a lead-in, but whatever one the teacher chooses, the main criteria is that the students are fully engaged with the topic rather than focusing on a specific language item or learning outcome. To do this, the teacher can use pictures, headlines, questions or statements for discussion. Students should then be given as much time as possible to use these prompts to offer ideas and opinions, make guesses or predictions or share personal stories and experiences. It helps if statements or discussion questions are open-ended and if pictures or headlines arouse curiosity, rather than merely depict the content of the lesson. In a sense, a good lead-in should be like a lesson itself in that it should create sufficient opportunities for communication, creativity and feedback on learner language. Of course, this depends on how much time the teacher has with the class and what they need to cover as part of the syllabus.

Helping learners process texts for meaning

A standard approach to working with texts in the language classroom is to set learners pre-prepared comprehension questions (eg. *Wh-* questions, multiple choice or true/false questions), which they need to answer while they read or listen to the text. These questions are generally designed to focus the learners' attention on the overall gist of the text or to enable them to locate specific pieces of information. However, comprehension questions found in a lot of teaching materials and coursebooks often merely test learners' recall of the text (Thornbury, 2006) or they target word or phrase level recognition (Field, 2008). This means that there is often only one correct answer to a question, thereby making it easier for the teacher to measure what the learners have understood or achieved. It is for this reason, perhaps, that comprehension questions, along with text summaries, are the most common methods for testing and assessing reading and listening skills in coursebooks, tests and examinations.

Yet comprehension questions can actually limit how much students are able to really think about and engage with the content of texts. Rather than focusing on the speaker's or writer's message and encouraging them to react to it, the learners are instead trying to extract specific chunks of information, often at the level of a single word or phrase. In addition, because the answers to comprehension questions are predetermined, the students are only focused on the parts of the text that the materials writer wants them to focus on (Roberts, 2014). As such, there is little room for students to make their own interpretations and discoveries or to focus on the parts of the text that interest them.

For this reason there is great value in designing questions or tasks that encourage the use of higher order thinking skills (Mishan & Timmis, 2015), as these will enable learners to interact more with what they read and listen to. Instead of only using questions that test basic understanding or recall (ie. lower order thinking skills), it is a good idea to encourage learners to make and defend judgements, understand arguments or link ideas found in texts to their experiences or personal or cultural values. Learners should also be encouraged to critique or review ideas, distinguish between facts and inferences, or to differentiate, organise or deconstruct the content of texts. These question or task types are not only extremely motivating, they can also take the lesson into unexpected territory. This cannot be done if there is only one right answer and students are only required to have a general understanding of what they read and listen to.

As well as designing questions or tasks that encourage learners to engage more with the content of texts, it is extremely beneficial for learners if the teacher also designs authentic tasks. This is especially true if the text itself is authentic or closely resembles an authentic genre or text type, that is, it appears to be authentic but has been adapted to suit the needs and interests of the students in the class. An authentic task, also called a real-world task (Tomlinson, 2011), should enable the learners to read or listen to the text for the same purpose as it would be read or listened to outside the classroom. For example, if learners are reading a review of a film, they should be asked if the review makes them want to watch it. If they are reading a discursive essay, they are asked if they agree or disagree with the opinions of the writer. As well as being a more realistic task, using authentic questions enables learners to read or listen more extensively outside the classroom because the question can be reused every time the learner meets the same text type. That way, as in the real world, the learners always have a purpose for reading or listening.

Using real-world tasks or questions that encourage learners to think more about the content of the text also prepares students for the language work that follows. In a typical text-based language lesson, comprehension questions help students to achieve 'a minimum level of understanding, without which any discussion of the target language would be pointless' (Thornbury, 1999). However, in order to enable the learners to understand and articulate the *reason* why a writer or speaker is using a certain form or forms, it is important to go beyond a basic understanding of the text. Instead, students need to fully understand the purpose of the text and the message the writer or the speaker wishes to convey. In other words, they need to be able to understand intended or pragmatic meanings as well as locating basic facts. Only then can learners be expected to understand why and how certain forms are being used.

Designing replication tasks

In the text-based lessons described in the teaching resources, the students are encouraged to work out for themselves why certain forms are being used by writers and speakers and how this helps them communicate their message successfully. Once this is done, it is then recommended that learners get the opportunity to use the language that they have uncovered, and an effective way for doing so is through the use of replication and transposition tasks. Yet before teachers design their own, it is necessary to consider what distinguishes these tasks from other types of practice activities.

First, replication and transposition tasks should encourage the students to use the target language for genuine communicative purposes. This means that rather than writing or completing individual sentences, the students create their own meanings at text level. It also means that rather than sticking solely to the target language, the students can integrate other known language into the task. In fact in some cases, it may be possible for students to complete the task successfully without using the target language.

In addition, a replication or transposition task should be a real-world task. This means that the students use the language in the same way and for the same purpose that it would be used outside the classroom. For example, the students might write a letter of complaint, attend a job interview or make a presentation. This means that replication and transposition tasks are open-ended: there is no one way of completing the task, and there will be different outcomes for different students. However, it is not necessary for teachers to only use tasks and content that their students are familiar with. Replication and transposition tasks should also enable students to be creative and to use language in unfamiliar or novel ways. This can then introduce students to new genres, new practices and different ways of thinking.

Finally, transposition and replication tasks should encourage learners to evaluate the reasons for using (or not using) a particular language item. Whether this is done in preparation for the task or during feedback, the learners should have time to ask themselves why they are using a given form and how it affects their message. That way, they gain a better understanding of reasons and how they help speakers and writers say what they want to say.

The following framework can be used as a guide for designing replication and transposition tasks. Of course, not all the criteria in this framework need to be achieved in every task that is designed. However, by using this checklist to ensure that some of the criteria are met, the learners are more likely to get genuine communicative practice as well as the opportunity to reflect on how they have used language to create their own meanings.

Criteria for task design	Replication tasks	Transposition tasks
Does the task enable the learners to use the target language in order to communicate a genuine message?	✓	✓
Does the task provide practice of the target language at text as opposed to sentence level?	✓	✓
Does the task allow the learners to integrate new language with other known language?	✓	✓
Does the task enable the students to use the language in the same way or for the same purpose as the speaker or writer of the original text?	✓	✗
Does the task reflect how language is used in the real world?	✓	✓
Is the task open-ended, ie. will there be different outcomes with different learners or groups of learners?	✓	✓
Does the task enable learners to explore language in unfamiliar areas?	✓	✓
Does the task allow for creativity?	✓	✓
Does the task enable the students to reflect on reasons either during preparation for the task or in feedback?	✓	✓

Note that in a transposition task, the students may not necessarily use an item of language in the same way or for the same purpose as the writer or speaker of the original text. For example, in a newspaper article, the writer might use indirect speech to report what people have said (eg. 'the company claimed that all their clients' details were secure'). If students were doing a replication task of this and writing their own article, they would be able to use indirect speech for the same purpose. However, in a transposition task in which the students were role-playing interviews between the journalist and someone mentioned in the article, it is possible that they will not need to use indirect speech at all. In feedback, learners can then discuss why indirect speech is used in one task type but not in another.

A planning template

When planning lessons and courses, it is important to design tasks that sufficiently challenge our students and enable them to think and act in different ways. The following template (Figure 3) is intended to be used for that purpose. Based on a design by Mishan and Timmis (2015), this template uses Bloom's taxonomy of thinking skills to help teachers categorise tasks according to their degree of challenge. By using this template, teachers can ensure that their students are provided with a sufficient range of variety and challenge in their classes.

Cognitive skill level and processes	Reading or listening tasks	Replication tasks	Transposition tasks
1. **Creating** *Students create new meanings and structures by reformulating content, building on ideas or hypothesising about causes, endings or outcomes.*			
2. **Evaluating** *Students make or defend judgements, link content to their own values, ideas and cultural background, or critique or review content.*			

Cognitive skill level and processes	Reading or listening tasks	Replication tasks	Transposition tasks
3. **Analysing** *Students separate facts from inference, deconstruct arguments, identify the relations between facts or organise or categorise.*			
4. **Applying** *Students reapply or change the content of the text to other contexts or situations by selecting or connecting ideas.*			
5. **Understanding** *Students interpret the message, paraphrase or describe it.*			
6. **Remembering** *Students recall data or information.*			

(Adapted from Mishan & Timmis, 2015)

How does this template work? Consider the following two sets of questions, designed to accompany the restaurant review found in the teaching resources (Lesson 1 on page 87).

Reading 1

1. What kind of restaurant is it?
2. What does the writer say about the atmosphere?
3. What food does the writer recommend?
4. Does the restaurant serve alcohol?
5. Do you need to book a table?

Reading 2

Would you eat in this restaurant? Why/why not?

Who would you go with? Why?

The first reading task uses comprehension questions that check students' understanding of facts or opinions that are stated directly in the text.

There is a right and a wrong answer to each question and very little room for discussion or disagreement about the answers. Because students are interpreting the message, these types of questions would be placed in **category 5** of the template.

The second reading task is more challenging, as it encourages the students to make their own judgements about the restaurant and to offer their own opinions. This task is far more open-ended, as the students need to provide reasons for whether they would eat at the restaurant and who they would choose to go with. Because these questions encourage students to make their own judgements and link the content to their own thoughts and experiences, they belong in **category 2**.

Using this template can help teachers prevent the issue described earlier in this section where it was shown that the kind of comprehension questions used in coursebooks often encourage students to use lower order thinking skills when reading or listening to texts. Where a coursebook predominantly uses these types of questions, it is possible that learners are subsequently under-challenged during comprehension work. If this is the case, teachers will need to create alternative tasks that would belong in the higher categories. This will then ensure that the students are provided with a suitable range of challenge in their lessons.

The template can also be used to categorise communicative tasks. In Task 1 below, because the students are encouraged to paraphrase or describe what they have read to their partner, this task would be placed in **category 5**. The second task is more challenging as the students now need to create their own text and express their own meanings. Because students are being creative, this task belongs in **category 1**.

Task 1

Student A: Read the review. When you have finished, tell your partner (student B) about it.

Task 2

Write your own review of a restaurant you have been to. Remember to describe the food, the atmosphere, the service and the price.

A lesson planning task

The planning template can also be used to help teachers develop planning skills. Using the following procedure and text, have a go at this yourself before moving on to the next section.

A lesson planning task

This task can be done individually or in a group of teachers or teachers in training.

- Read the text below from Chapter 3 about the man who smuggled animal parts into the UK.
- Either working alone or with a group of colleagues, use the planning template to brainstorm as many comprehension, replication and transposition tasks for this text as you can. You do not need to use every category, and do not worry too much about which box each activity goes in.
- Once you have finished, decide on which ones you think would make the best lesson.
- When you are ready, compare your ideas with those in the completed template below (Figure 4).

You can then do the same activity with a text you regularly use with your students or with one from your current coursebook.

Police make wild discovery in airport luggage

A 50-year-old Londoner has been arrested at a UK airport for attempting to bring body parts, bones and eggs from a range of protected species into the country in his luggage. After being stopped and questioned by airport police and customs officials, commercial premises belonging to the man's family were searched and various illegal items were seized and taken away for testing. Amongst a large haul of uncertified items, police found turtle shells and eggs as well as bottles of snake wine, a drink believed to have restorative and curative powers in many parts of Asia.

The smuggled wildlife were listed as endangered by CITES (Convention on International Trade in Endangered Species), and the seized animals will be handed over to the Department of the Environment to establish if they can be returned to their country of origin.

The accused, who claimed the animals were for private collections and gifts, has been released on bail pending further enquiries.

Figure 4

Cognitive skill level and processes	Reading or listening tasks	Replication tasks	Transposition tasks
1. **Creating** *Students create new meanings and structures by reformulating content, building on ideas or hypothesising about causes, endings or outcomes.*	■ Ask students why the man did it and what he was going to do next. ■ Students write their own questions before reading the text. ■ Create back-stories for the man.	■ Rewrite the text with the police as the subject. ■ Learners write their own article using an alternative headline.	■ Role-play an interview between the police and the smuggler. ■ Role-play an interview between a journalist and the man or the police. ■ Transpose the text to another medium, eg. a report on the news or an eyewitness account. ■ Rewrite the text from the man's perspective. ■ Rewrite the text from the perspective of the police.
2. **Evaluating** *Students make or defend judgements, link content to their own values, ideas and cultural background, or critique or review content.*	■ Students decide what punishment the man should receive. ■ Students discuss what punishments the man is likely to receive. ■ Students discuss why smuggling animals and animal parts is a serious crime. ■ Students discuss what might happen in their country.		■ Split class so they argue for strong and lenient punishments.

Cognitive skill level and processes	Reading or listening tasks	Replication tasks	Transposition tasks
3. **Analysing** *Students separate facts from inference, deconstruct arguments, identify the relations between facts or organise or categorise.*	■ Students separate facts from claims. ■ Students brainstorm possible reasons why people smuggle. ■ Students discuss why the article made the news.		
4. **Applying** *Students reapply or change the content of the text to other contexts or situations by selecting or connecting ideas.*			■ Transpose the text to another medium eg. a news report or witness account.
5. **Understanding** *Students interpret the message, paraphrase or describe it.*	■ Students answer comprehension questions with *what, where* etc. ■ Learners summarise the text (with or without prompts). ■ Learners add information to timelines, tables or forms. ■ Students correct an incorrect summary. ■ Learners locate and highlight facts in the text, eg. dates, times, names etc.	■ Students reconstruct the text from prompts. ■ Students do a dictogloss activity from part of the text. ■ Students do translation or re-translation activities.	
6. **Remembering** *Students recall data or information.*	■ Students re-answer comprehension questions with *what, where* etc. ■ Students reorder a cut-up text. ■ Ask students what they can remember.		

As you can see, there are many different things that students can do with this text. The key is to choose the activities that you believe your students will find the most interesting and stimulating or those that enable them to practise the skills that they need. It is also important to ensure that over a series of lessons, the students get a suitable range of task types and are encouraged to think and act in different ways. Although it is at times difficult to choose exactly which category a task goes into, the template above can help teachers to do that.

Conclusion

As Tomlinson (2011) suggests, the techniques and procedures outlined here should be viewed as informative rather than prescriptive. They should be used to provide teachers with a menu of profitable ideas and options as opposed to a strict framework for every lesson. Ultimately, it is the teacher and the students who should have control over the content of lessons and courses, the order in which they do things and the pace of their lessons (Maley, 2011). However, in order to help teachers make informed decisions about how to incorporate specific techniques and approaches into their syllabuses, it is useful to work from a set of guiding principles. This will now be explored in the next and final section of the book.

Section 3

Teaching and training implications

'I'm not afraid to use the word grammar, but I can see why people would be.'
David Crystal

The previous sections outlined an alternative approach to working with grammar in the language classroom. This section asks and answers questions arising from this in order to:

■ explore the principles underpinning the approaches and techniques outlined in previous chapters

■ look at ways of incorporating the approach on different courses

■ suggest how the approaches and techniques can be used for training new and inexperienced teachers

■ include comments from students, teachers and teacher developers, and explore the implications of these views.

What principles underpin the approach?

Tomlinson (2011) suggests that materials, approaches and techniques should be underpinned by a set of principles which may either be applicable to all types of classes, or be relevant to a specific local context. In terms of the approaches and techniques found in this book, five main principles apply.[1]

1. **Learners should be exposed to rich, varied and meaningful input that is relevant to their needs, interests, culture and social context.** In the procedures and materials described in this book, exposure to meaningful language comes in the form of written and spoken texts. These texts can be both authentic, in that they have not been written for the purpose of studying a language, or graded, that is, created specifically for the L2 classroom. Texts can also be

---

1   The principles outlined in this section were drawn from a range of applied linguists and materials writers, e.g. Krashen (1982), Swain (1985), Nation (1996), Ellis (2008), Dörnyei (2009) Tomlinson (2011) and Hadfield (2015).

created by the learners themselves or by other students. For example, the teacher might use pieces of student writing or a recording of a group of learners performing a communicative task. In addition, students should be encouraged to find interesting texts that they would like to explore in the classroom.

2. **Comprehension tasks should encourage learners to be analytical and evaluative. They should encourage learners to think for themselves as often as possible.** As discussed in Section 2, Part 2, a lot of comprehension questions found in coursebooks and teaching materials lack challenge, and students are often led to the parts of the text the materials writer wants them to focus on. The upshot of this is that reading and listening stages can be quite mechanical, and students are often left with an incomplete understanding of the content. To prevent this from happening, learners should instead be encouraged to react to what they read and listen to. This can be done by asking them to draw conclusions, make inferences and judgements, or seek possible causes or consequences. Because the outcome of these reading and listening tasks is open-ended rather than predetermined, what students take from the text will not be the same for every class and teaching context.

3. **Learners benefit from noticing specific examples of language and working out for themselves why they are being used by the writer or speaker(s).** A central principle underpinning this approach is that learners should be encouraged to think for themselves, as a lot of learning takes place through exploration and discovery (Willis, 2003). For this reason, learners should be prompted to notice examples of language, either through input materials or from speaking or writing tasks. Once they have done this, students should be encouraged to work out the reason why specific forms are being used. Of course the forms the learners explore can be chosen by the teacher in advance, but learners should be equally able to focus on areas of language that *they* want to explore, whether grammar, lexis or features of spoken or written discourse. This means that teachers do not need to stick to specific lesson aims, and time should be set aside for questions and digressions.

4. **Learners should be encouraged to use language meaningfully and creatively in order to communicate their own messages and ideas.** Whether in response to texts or during communicative tasks, lessons and courses should include extensive opportunities

for students to use new forms to express their own meanings. Where possible, practice activities should enable students to use new language for communicative purposes as opposed to simply recalling or repeating what they have studied through mechanical drills or simple transformation or gap-filling exercises. In addition, it is a good idea to encourage students to use new language in creative or unfamiliar ways. This enables learners to express themselves in ways they have not done before, thereby helping them to go beyond their present level of learning. This is thought to lead students to deeper and more durable learning (Tomlinson, 2011).

5. **Learners should be encouraged to notice gaps and to reflect on successful language use**. Helping students to move outside their comfort zone and encouraging them to use language in new and challenging ways puts students in a better position to notice gaps in their language knowledge (Thornbury, 2006). Once learners have noticed a gap, they are then in a better position to upgrade what they want to say or are struggling to say. Even if they are not quite ready to do so, noticing a gap enables learners to consciously recognise any linguistic problems they are having. This gives both the teacher and the learner something to work on, either during the lesson or later in the course.

Are there other important principles that teachers should consider?

As this is a book about grammar and grammar teaching, the approaches and techniques outlined in the previous chapters are designed to help learners develop a better understanding of specific grammatical items. The materials found in Section 2 therefore all contain some degree of grammatical focus. However, the approach, techniques and materials are not meant to be viewed as the basis of a grammatical syllabus, as this would give the learners an incomplete view of the language and a narrow set of skills. For this reason it is important to consider one other key principle when creating materials and designing courses.

6. **Learners need to be exposed to and develop a wide repertoire of collocations, phrases and formulaic and functional expressions**.

Formulaic expressions are groups of words that have a specific meaning or function. For example, *I see what you mean* is often used to signal understanding or agreement, while *I see what you're saying, but ...* is a very common way of signalling polite disagreement. This kind of language is extremely widespread, and the meaning or function of what we say or write is often carried in the formulaic expressions we use (Wray, 2002). So it is clear that students should be helped to develop a range of formulaic expressions as early as possible.

The same is true for collocations. A lack of knowledge of collocations has been shown to cause comprehension problems and it is widely accepted that if L2 learners want to use language accurately and fluently, they need to know and use a wide range of acceptable collocations (Fernández & Schmitt, 2015). For this reason, a syllabus focusing solely on grammar is not recommended.

Can the approach and techniques described in this book be used to explore lexis or other aspects of language?

The approaches described in this book encourage learners to explore the reasons why a writer or speaker uses a specific form to communicate their message, and the same approach can be used to look at words or phrases. In fact, it can even be used to determine why a speaker might use a certain tone or stress a specific word.

Consider the following short extract, taken from a cable TV show broadcast in the USA. In the programme, the speaker argues that he does not agree with celebrities who talk about political issues because their wealth and privilege means that they do not have a sufficient understanding of the problem. It is an interesting argument and a great topic to explore with adult and young adult learners. It is also a very interesting text in terms of the language the speaker uses and the way he speaks.

Celebrities, I don't really <u>care</u>. You know, quite <u>hon</u>estly, when cel<u>eb</u>rities sound <u>off</u> about politics, when cel<u>eb</u>rities <u>TAKE</u> a stand, <u>I</u> tune out.

(Underlined sections indicate the stressed syllables)

© Artisan news service 2010

In terms of lexis, it is interesting to explore the reason why the speaker uses the phrase *sound off about politics* rather than *talk about politics*. Where *talk about* is quite neutral, the phrase *sound off* shows how the speaker views the action. When you *sound off* about something, you express your views quite forcefully and loudly, often without being invited to do so. It is actually quite close to the word *complain*. The speaker here is using the phrase because it has negative connotations. It is interesting to note that later in the show he uses the term *speak up* to describe his own activism. This word carries the notion of expressing support for someone or something in difficult circumstances and by using it, the speaker creates the impression that when he talks about political issues, it is brave and noble.

The second interesting point is how he uses the collocation *take a stand*. This phrase usually describes someone's positive efforts to resist or fight for something, for example, *take a stand against racism*. It is often used with *must*, *have to* or *should*. However, the speaker places a heavy stress on the word *take*. By doing so, he comes across as sarcastic and mocking of what the celebrities are doing, which shows how speakers can use stress and intonation to make a positive expression sound negative.

As with grammar, in order to help learners better understand these concepts, the teacher can use the same frame as suggested in Section 1, Chapter 3. For example:

Why is the speaker using the phrase *sound off about politics*
rather than *talk about politics*?
Why does the speaker emphasise the word *take* in *take a stand*?

By using these frames, teachers can help students explore lexical items and aspects of phonology with the same critical eye that they use to analyse grammar.

Can lower level students formulate reasons?

Whenever learners process texts for meaning or take part in communicative tasks, it is possible to encourage them to reflect on the reasons behind the use of specific language items. Of course this is more difficult for lower level students, who lack the skills to describe reasons, but if the concept is simple enough, it can be done. However, before deciding when students are ready to start looking at language in this way, it is necessary to consider when L2 learners should begin studying grammar in the first place.

For example, there are persuasive reasons why grammar should not be taught to beginners. First, immersion studies have shown that many learners are able to acquire basic word order skills and important inflections such as the *-ed* ending of past simple verbs without overt teaching or assistance. In fact, many learners can go a long way without focused input. Although there is the danger of fossilisation, where an L2 error becomes a permanent part of a learner's language, it seems that grammar acquisition in the early stages takes place naturally and inevitably. This suggests that the key is to provide learners with plenty of exposure to the L2 and extensive opportunities to use it (Ellis, 2002b). In order to prevent fossilisation, the teacher intervenes with corrections or reformulations, but does not overtly focus on the form.

Ellis also suggests that as with L1 acquisition, a lot of early learning is naturally ungrammatical. Instead, L2 students begin by learning and using lots of words and formulaic expressions. They then start to construct their own sequences in order to convey meaning, for example, *I no understand* or *What means xxx*? As the learners progress, they begin to refine their messages by adding grammar and complexity. Because the early stages of language acquisition are lexical rather than grammatical, this suggests that a lot of instruction at lower levels should have a lexical focus.

As learners make progress and start processing longer and more authentic texts or doing more extensive communicative tasks, they will naturally need to use or understand more complex areas of language. When this happens, it is beneficial to encourage learners to start working out the reasons why certain items of language are being used. The benefits of this have been extensively covered in Section 1, Chapter 3, but for lower levels, one advantage of this approach is that the students do not need to know

Teaching Grammar: From Rules to Reasons © Pavilion Publishing and Media Ltd and its licensors 2016.

specific grammar terminology in order to formulate reasons. They simply use their own words. The other significant benefit of using this approach at lower levels is that it encourages students to start working things out for themselves at the earliest possible opportunity.

However, it is important to consider that discovering and formulating reasons is not an easy thing for students to do straightaway. Teachers need to guide students, as they would in any discovery task. For example, on the first occasion that lower level learners explore reasons, they could be given a set of options and have to choose the best one. They then start formulating their own reasons when they are ready. In monolingual classes, lower level students can also formulate reasons in their own L1. As Bolitho (2011) suggests, using L1 to think and talk about English should not be seen as a problem. It is the quality of the thinking and talking that counts.

In what other ways can students use their L1?

Another way of exploiting the learners' L1 is to use a technique known as reverse translation for the replication task. This works in the following way. As in the text-based lessons described in Section 2, the learners begin by processing a short text for meaning. Once this is done, the teacher hands out copies of the text translated into the students' L1. They then work in pairs or small groups to retranslate the text back into English.

The aim of reverse translation is not to encourage students to reproduce an original text word-for-word. Instead, it provides opportunities for students to notice features of the language they are learning and to discover gaps between their first language and the L2. The collaborative work encourages students to think about the process of working between languages and enables them to negotiate meaning as they choose the most appropriate forms (Kerr, 2014).

This procedure works well for monolingual groups where the teacher speaks or has some knowledge of the students' L1. However, this is not entirely necessary, as the teacher does not need to know the students L1 in order to assess the quality of their retranslations. In fact, for a native English-speaking teacher (NEST) working with a monolingual group, reverse translation can teach them something about the language their students speak.

Although it is slightly more difficult to manage, reverse translation can also be used with multilingual groups. In order to do this, the students follow up the comprehension work by translating the original text into their L1. After a delay, they then work together to retranslate it back into English. In a multilingual classroom, students enjoy finding similarities and differences between their languages and explaining to each other what they find difficult about learning English. As well as being an interesting discussion, it helps to build rapport between the students, as they develop a greater awareness of each other's languages, cultures and learning needs. As with monolingual groups, reverse translation can help the teacher learn something about their students' languages.

It is also possible to use materials that have already been translated into multiple languages, and for a rich source of short, engaging and authentic listening texts that come with translations, teachers do not need to look much further than TED talks. Found at www.ted.com, these are a series of short, informative and educational lectures given by some of the world's leading thinkers and innovators. As there are currently over a hundred talks on the site, it is not surprising that this is now one of the most popular sources of texts for teachers worldwide.

How can the technique be used with coursebooks?

Although the use of coursebooks in the language classroom continues to divide opinion, they are often used by language schools to provide a framework for courses or to act as the syllabus for different levels. In addition, teachers frequently use them as a source of material, activities and ideas. While Section 1, Chapter 2 discusses the issues with the way that coursebooks frequently describe grammar and provide practice of language items, the approaches and techniques described in Section 1, Chapter 3 offer alternative ways that teachers can use their coursebooks. These are detailed below.

- Teachers can replace comprehension questions with more open-ended, evaluative questions. This will encourage learners to interact with the content more and generate discussion.

■ Learners can formulate reasons for the way that language is used by writers and speakers of texts. This means that students will be able to notice uses of language items that are not typically covered in coursebooks. However, it is important to ensure that the language in the text is natural, as graded reading texts or scripted dialogues written specifically for the level can often be unnatural or artificial. Texts might also be included purely to present a language item. This can mean that not only is it difficult for students to relate to the materials, which can stifle any possible discussion about the content, but it can also make it difficult for learners to uncover genuine, communicative reasons. Instead, they are being led to 'discover' the rule. The following approaches and techniques can help teach us the vary the way they use their coursebooks:

  ■ The teacher can use replication or transposition tasks to provide more communicative practice of language items. This type of practice is more likely to lead to spontaneous and meaningful use of the target language than the type of controlled practice activities often found in coursebooks.

  ■ By using genuinely communicative tasks, the teacher can work with what emerges and with language forms that are not included in the coursebook syllabus.

As well as providing teachers with different ways of working, more importantly perhaps, these approaches can help teachers to develop a more critical view of the materials they use and the way that language is frequently presented to their students. The learners also have more space and opportunities to make genuine discoveries for themselves.

Does the approach allow for the kind of controlled practice activities found in coursebooks?

One of the principles underpinning the approach outlined in earlier chapters is that students should be encouraged to use language meaningfully and creatively in order to communicate their own messages and ideas. This is not provided by controlled practice activities such as gap-fills, drills or complete-the-sentence exercises. For this reason, it is recommended that students create their own texts and meanings by doing replication or transposition tasks.

However, this does not mean that controlled practice activities should not be used. Many adult learners set themselves high standards of accuracy, and controlled practice can provide much needed confidence for this type of learner. In addition, controlled practice can help raise students' awareness of language patterns that might otherwise go unnoticed in freer practice tasks or during reading and listening stages. It is also thought that repetition in the form of drills can help students commit language patterns to working memory (eg. Bilborough, 2013). With further repetition, exposure and opportunities to use new forms, it is more likely that these items will subsequently be retained. Most importantly, it is believed that repetition and controlled practice activities can lead to automaticity, the ability to use or understand language without conscious effort or attention. The key, therefore, is to design activities that are relevant, engaging and motivating (Arnold *et al*, 2015), and to remember that controlled practice and focused attention on specific language items is largely ineffective without communication.

Can the approach be used in exam classes?

As seen in Lesson 8 (the discursive essay on page 111), the approach can be used to develop students' knowledge of the types of written text that they will need to produce in their exams. Because the approach is collaborative in nature, it can help motivate students to do writing tasks in class rather than for homework. This subsequently enables the teacher to be on hand to answer questions about language, provide lexis that the learners need and to help them structure sentences and organise information in a more natural or appropriate way. In terms of spoken texts, students can listen to recordings of other learners or proficient speakers doing exam tasks before exploring the reasons behind the use of specific grammatical forms, lexical items or aspects of spoken discourse. Once they are ready, the students can have a go at doing the task themselves.

For listening and reading skills, replication tasks can be used to help develop learners' ability to summarise texts, which is a common exam task. However, exam students need to develop techniques for answering the types of comprehension questions typically used in tests, such as matching, true/false questions or multiple choice exercises. In addition, students may need to do specific controlled practice activities that demonstrate that they can use language accurately. This means they need to practise and develop strategies for doing gap-fills, sentence transformation activities or cloze activities (completing a text by adding words in gaps) if these types of exercise are found in the test. Therefore, the approach and techniques outlined in this book will need to be supplemented with exam training and practice of the types of exercises used in language tests.

Can the approach be combined with progress tests and assessments?

The main aim of the approach outlined in this book is to create opportunities for learning to occur. Through exposure to rich and varied input, a conscious focus on language items, active and meaningful use of the language, and feedback on performance, learning opportunities are maximised. Because the approach does not rest on the assumption that students learn what is taught in the order it is taught, there is no specific need for the teacher to set the students tangible language-related goals that are tested at the end of the course.

Before a course begins, however, the teacher and students might identify relevant functions, tasks and text types that are appropriate to the level or the learners' real-life context. Assessment would then be focused on how effectively students are able to carry out these tasks and functions. If this is the case, the teacher might devise a set of criteria to measure how successful the learners have been. This may include such areas as successful completion of the task, appropriacy of style, communicative ability, and the level of accuracy or range of structures used. These areas could be rated on a scale from 1 to 10. Alternatively, students can be given individual feedback on general strengths and weaknesses.

Because evidence of progress is thought to be a strong motivating factor for language learners, it is important that students are given regular feedback on their performance. If a course does not have a set of specific goals, students still need to be made aware of their progress and development. This can be done through individual feedback sessions, private tutorials or through the use of reports. Learners can also be encouraged to monitor their own progress, perhaps through the use of learning journals. Additionally, learners can be encouraged to set themselves realistic goals and work towards achieving them. These can subsequently be explored in tutorials or open-class discussions.

To sum up, if teachers choose not to include formal tests on their courses, students still need to be able to reflect on success and be made aware of what needs to improve.

Can the approaches and techniques be used on ESP (English for Specific Purposes) courses?

The approaches and techniques outlined in previous chapters are very suitable for ESP courses. This is due to the fact that ESP focuses more on how language is used in specific contexts than on teaching grammar and language structures independently. As such, reading, listening and noticing tasks can be used to help raise learners' awareness of relevant spoken and written genres, while replication tasks enable students to practise communicating in the way they would outside class. The key is to choose appropriate texts and tasks that meet the specific needs of the learners. For example, students studying for business purposes can listen to people negotiating in English and explore how the discussion is structured. They can then perform the task themselves. Likewise, students on EAP courses (English for Academic Purposes) can work towards developing essay-writing skills or giving presentations on their research.

On ESP courses for professionals, students are not developing new skills or exploring new genres but learning how to do familiar tasks in English. The fact that students already have a sound knowledge of their subject matter enhances their ability to explore reasons. This subsequently enables them to match language items to their function more effectively than students on more general English language programmes, which makes the approaches and techniques outlined previously very appropriate for ESP courses.

What do you do if students cannot formulate a reason or if they rely on an existing rule?

The motivation L2 learners get from discovering something new cannot be overestimated, and it is thought that learners understand and remember better when they have worked things out for themselves (eg. Ellis & Shintani, 2014). There is therefore a sound rationale for using inductive approaches in the L2 classroom, despite the fact that there will inevitably be occasions when the learners are unable to work out the meaning or recognise a pattern without help. This is especially true if the technique the teacher uses is unfamiliar.

The key is to create a culture of enquiry and to make students comfortable with the fact that they will occasionally get things wrong or struggle to work something out. When this happens, the teacher needs to be on hand to guide learners and help them formulate their own reasons. If they cannot, the teacher can simply tell them.

As well as leading to more memorable and durable learning, exploring and formulating reasons can help learners to view grammar in a different way. This can be seen in comments made by Soo, a student at the end of a four-week course at intermediate level (B1), in which the learners were encouraged to explore reasons rather than rules.

'Before I never thinking about the why. Why this grammar? I just studied grammar and learnt this grammar is a rule. Just a rule. But after thinking about the why, why this sentence using *will* or passive, so I start to think about the grammar and maybe I try to make the rule (reason) in my mind. It's difficult but it's good.' **Soo, South Korea**

Despite the fact that Soo admits that it was difficult at times, the technique has had two significant outcomes. Where she previously only studied the rule, she has begun to think about why certain forms are used. This is the first time she has done this in her learning experience. Second, she has started to create her own descriptions of meaning as she studies English. These two positive outcomes clearly outweigh the fact that she will not always get things right the first time.

What are the benefits of using the approach on training courses for new

or inexperienced teachers?

First, the lessons and the planning template in Section 2, Part 2 can be used to help new teachers or teachers in training (trainees) design their own lessons. This can be done in the following way:

1. The trainer demos the lesson with the trainees acting as the students. Alternatively, they could show a video of a teacher using the approach, or the trainees could observe the trainer teaching a live lesson.

2. At the end, the trainer and trainees unpack the lesson. They do this by discussing the order of the lesson and the rationale behind each stage.

3. The trainer hands out an interesting text. Once the trainees have read the text, they form pairs or small groups. They then use the planning template in Section 2 in order to create as many lead-ins, comprehension tasks and replication/transposition tasks as they can within a time limit. As they work together, the trainer monitors the trainees, offering guidance.

4. Ideas are gathered together in open-class feedback. Alternatively, the trainees can present their ideas to the rest of the class.

5. If possible, the trainees teach their lessons with practice students or in a micro-teaching session with their peers. The trainer can observe the lesson and provide feedback.

6. Once they have done this, the trainer and trainees can discuss what language items might be looked at and how this could be done.

This session demonstrates to trainees that with a simple formula, they are able to create a number of interesting and engaging lessons in a short space of time. It also encourages trainees to be creative. This can be extremely motivating, as Norma, a trainee on a teacher training course in 2014, attests.

'It may be a personal thing, some teachers like to have prompts and guidelines that they can follow but for me, creating a lesson from a text, a free text, was more interesting and stimulating. It's about using your creativity, letting things flow and not being too confined.' **Norma, UK**

As well as encouraging creativity, the approach can be used to reduce the fear that trainees have about teaching grammar. Many trainees on pre-service courses such as the Cambridge CELTA (Certificate of English Language Teaching to Adults) and the Trinity Cert TESOL (Certificate in Teaching English to Speakers of Other Languages) suggest that grammar is the thing that causes them the most concern. Many also suggest that they find it difficult to find and understand the rules. This seems to be especially true for many native speaker teachers who have never had to study the grammar of English.

By encouraging trainees to explore reasons rather than rules, they are able to see that grammar is not merely a network of rules to be learnt and taught, but a system that writers and speakers use to express meaning. Because they are able to understand what writers and speakers mean, they are able to work out the reasons behind their use of specific forms. After using this approach on their courses, trainees have commented on the fact that grammar became more logical and less intimidating than they first thought. It has also helped trainees to become more comfortable when answering students' questions about language or working with emerging or unplanned language. This is because rather than feeling that they need to know a rule or think of it on the spot, they know that they can work together with the students to discover the meaning and why the speaker or writer is using the form. They can then look up the rule later. This can go on to inform their style of teaching, as attested by Elizabeth, who made the following comment shortly after completing her CELTA and going to work in Italy.

'It didn't really impact on the course ... but I now deal with emerging language every day. I always enjoy this aspect of teaching, as discovering meaning together always leads to a nice "eureka" moment.' **Elizabeth, UK**

Brown (2014) suggests that, 'If effective on-the-spot clarification and improvisation in the classroom are qualities that experienced teachers have, surely these are qualities we should encourage in trainee teachers'. By exploring reasons on training courses, trainee and newly qualified teachers are developing these qualities straightaway.

Finally, the approaches and techniques outlined in the book can help trainee teachers to become less reliant on published materials. This is done by training them to exploit texts and design tasks, as well as instilling the confidence to work with emerging language more. In addition, by looking at how they can adapt coursebooks and considering alternative ways of exploring and using new language, trainees can become better able to identify and compensate for deficits in the materials available to teachers, which according to Bolitho (2015) is a necessary part of a teacher training course.

For more experienced teachers working towards higher level qualifications such as the Cambridge and Trinity diplomas or those attending short language development courses, analysing reasons is an effective way of developing their existing language awareness. However, as Christine, a teacher and teacher developer working in the UK, states, trainers need to be aware that teachers who are comfortable with their knowledge of the rules may be reluctant to explore language in a different way.

> '[There were] some English teachers who felt very confident that they knew the rules about how various verb forms are used and had become a little complacent in this. Therefore, they didn't try to look inside themselves for their own personal thoughts or interpretations about why the writers/speakers made their language choices.' **Christine, UK**

This is something to factor in when introducing the approach onto courses with more experienced teachers.

Conclusion

This book does not seek to place grammar at the centre of our courses and syllabuses. It suggests instead that teachers need to look at and teach grammar differently. To do this, it should not be viewed as a fixed system of rules that students will acquire one-by-one. Grammar is far more dynamic. It is a tool that different speakers and writers use to convey their meaning in different situations. Rather than strictly following the rules, speakers and writers make choices. It is these choices that L2 learners should explore.

By exploiting texts and tasks in the classroom, students can better understand meaning and language use through exploring the reasons why writers and speakers use specific items of grammar to say what they want to say. This will in turn give learners a greater appreciation of the role of grammar and help them use it more effectively and purposefully in genuine communicative situations.

Teacher's notes

Lesson 2: Jade and Sam

She would come to my home and <u>she'd be sitting</u>
behind me when I was playing games.

This student's example seems unusual at first, as the form *would be + -ing* is most commonly used to describe an action that is already in progress by the time another action begins, as in the original text when Jade writes *I'd visit him at his home and he'd be sitting in front of his computer*. This meaning can be demonstrated with a timeline.

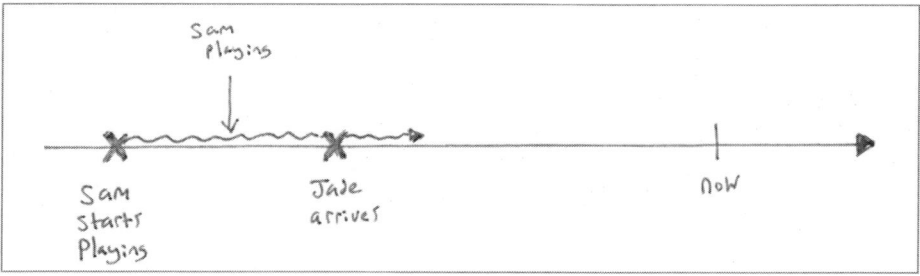

However, this is not the case in the student's example. The student was trying to describe a sequence of events that happened '<u>while</u> he was playing games'. In this instance, it would be useful to demonstrate how *would + infinitive* or the *past simple* can be used to show a sequence like this. Again, a timeline would help make the meaning clearer.

- *She would come to my home and she'd sit behind me.*

- *She would come to my home and sit behind me.*

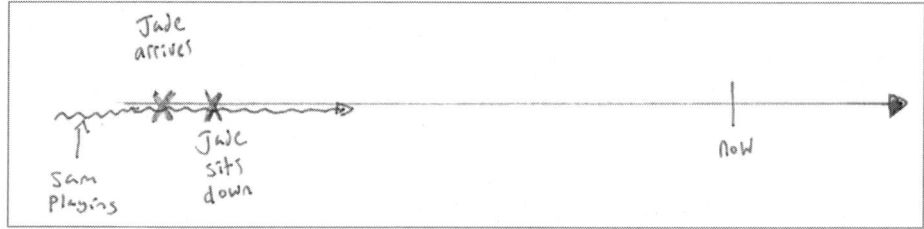

It's worth noting that *would be + -ing* can sometimes be used to express irritation with someone's past actions, so the sentence *She would come to my home and she'd be sitting behind me when I was playing games* is not grammatically wrong if this meaning is intended. This different use of *would be + -ing* could be explored in feedback.

Lesson 3: By the time I get to Phoenix

By the time I get to Pittsburgh she'll be partying
She'll listen to our song and start to cry ††

One of the advantages of using replication and transposition tasks is that even though the students might be using the grammar accurately and appropriately, they may still need guidance with certain lexical items. In this instance, the student has used *listen to* when they wanted to use *hear*.

The reason is due to the fact that when you *listen to* something it is a more intentional and deliberate act. When you *hear* something, it is not intentional. It just happens. The following two examples demonstrate the difference.

> *By the time I get to Pittsburgh she'll be partying*
> *She'll hear our song and start to cry.*

In this example, because the girl is at a party, she hears their song because it happens to be playing. She did not chose to play it or to listen to it. When the song starts playing, she starts to cry. This is the meaning that the student wanted to express.

In the following example, however, the act of listening is far more deliberate. It suggests that the girl puts on their song and listens to it. She then starts to cry.

> *By the time I get to Pittsburgh she'll be sitting alone at home*
> *She'll listen to our song and start to cry.*

She'll cut all my pictures and letters. ††

In this example, the student needed to use the collocation *cut up* rather than *cut*.

Lesson 4: The wild discovery

Because first he introduce the man then he wants to keep focus on the man ††

The journalist possibly chooses to make the smuggler the focus of the article because he is the most newsworthy aspect of the story. The reader will be more interested in what he was doing and what was in his luggage than the police arresting him. Once the journalist has chosen the man as the point of interest in the story, he then uses the passive to maintain the focus on the man and to introduce new information, for example, the fact that the police stopped, searched and arrested him.

This does not then suggest that the police are 'unimportant'. The man was simply chosen as the more interesting angle for the story. Therefore the writer introduced him first. This would be a useful area to explore.

Lesson 5: The internet ban

The man says it's not all the kids it's only <u>part of the kids</u> in the library ††

This is an interesting error. The learner understands why the relative clause is being used by the speaker. However, they have struggled to form it themselves. The following reformulation would therefore help the learner use a relative clause more accurately in their reason.

> *The man says it's not all the kids in the village.*
> *It is only <u>the ones that use the library.</u>*

Lesson 6: The election pledge

The students <u>can drink coffee</u> during the lesson ††

Though this sentence is grammatically accurate, it does not sound like the kind of pledge a politician would make. Along with the use of the definite article and singular noun (the lesson) it sounds as if the students are getting permission to drink coffee in one particular class. The following example is therefore more appropriate.

> *Students <u>will be able to drink coffee</u> during lessons.*
> *or*
> *Students <u>will be allowed to drink coffee</u> during lessons.*

Lesson 8: The discursive essay

Although <u>this transformation</u> has been extremely positive …
… <u>this means</u> that young people feel they need to have the newest model.
<u>This</u> can only be bad news for society.

In this essay, the writer is using the determiner *this* to refer back to ideas, words and phrases that have already been mentioned in the text. It can also be used to avoid repeating words, phrases or complete sentences.

In the classroom, the teacher can raise awareness of this type of referencing by asking the students to identify who or what the pronouns in a text refer to. They can also compare texts that contain effective referencing and minimal repetition with ones that do not. In terms of providing practice, students use pronouns to replace words or phrases.

Although <u>this transformation</u> has been extremely positive …

'*this transformation*' refers back to the idea that '*our lives have been completely transformed*' in the previous sentence. Changing a verb phrase (*have been transformed*) into a noun (*this transformation*) in this is known as nominalisation, which is a common feature of academic writing.

… <u>this means</u> that young people feel they need to have the newest model.

In this example, *this* refers back to the phrase '*Smartphones have also become must-have accessories*' in the previous sentence. The writer uses *this* to introduce the consequences of smart-phones being a must-have accessory. By replacing the whole phrase with a determiner, the writer is able to be succinct and avoid repetition.

<u>This</u> can only be bad news for society.

Here, *this* refers back to the idea that because of the influence of smartphones, society will become more closed and selfish over time. Again, the writer uses the linking word to introduce a new idea, to avoid repetition and to be succinct.

Lesson 11: Student dilemmas

If + would is less easy choice. †† There is more change.

Though the reason that the students have created is very perceptive, it would be useful to reformulate it so that they can express the idea more clearly. This can be seen in the following recommendations.

> Jay is using **If + would** to show that this option is more difficult. Jay will need to make more lifestyle changes if he chooses it.
>
> or
>
> They are using **If + would** to show that this option is more difficult. Going to the USA will be a bigger change than staying in Taiwan.

Lesson 12: The magic camera

Timelines are a very effective way of demonstrating the order or length of events. The following timeline can be used alongside these learner-generated reasons to help them better understand how.

We <u>were driving back</u> to the exit of the national park.
We <u>hadn't really seen</u> anything all day.
Suddenly this elephant just <u>appeared</u> and started smashing up a tree right in front of us.

- the past continuous '*is the background to the story. It takes us to the beginning of the story*'

- the past simple '*takes us forward*'

- the past perfect simple '*takes us back if we need to go back. It tells us about the time before you take the photo.*'

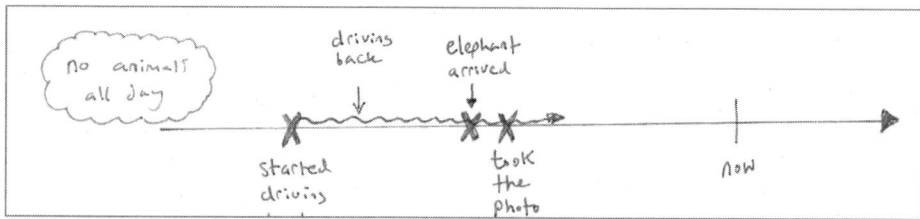

Lesson 14: The balloon debate

Should is my opinion and idea. It shows a good idea to choose me. ††
If shows future possibility for why keep the doctor. People will be sick. ††
Can't shows no good ability for the judge is why we don't keep him. ††

Each of these learner-generated reasons is an appropriate description of the meaning. However, it would be useful to reformulate these reasons so that the students have a clearer and more accurate example to record in their notebooks. Reformulation can also introduce useful collocations such as *give an opinion*.

> *We are using **should** to give our opinions.*
> *We think that it is a good idea to choose me.*
>
> **If** *is a future possibility. It gives a reason for why we should keep the doctor.*
>
> *We are using **can't** because the judge does not have useful abilities for the island. It gives a reason why we shouldn't keep him.*

Lesson 17: What happened?

It's the past but we don't know what happen. ††

It is thought that many lower level learners are able to acquire basic word order skills and important inflections such as the *-ed* ending of past simple verbs without overt teaching or assistance. However, when learners make errors such as the one above, the teacher can help learners notice the form by intervening and reformulating. In fact, the learners could also be asked why the speaker needed to use *-ed* at the end of the verb. The reason is simple; it is because they are speaking about the past.

> *It's the past but we don't know what happened.*

Lesson 18: Battersea Power Station Part 2

We think a music venue <u>would be</u> really popular.

In this example, the student is giving a reason for their choice. They are describing a possible benefit of turning the power station into a music venue.

<u>If we create</u> a music venue, <u>it'll promote</u> the arts and bring tourists to this part of London.

In this example of the first conditional, the student is again giving a reason for their choice. However, by using *will* the speaker sounds more certain about the outcome.

<u>Yes, but</u> that's not going to bring in any money.

The student is using the phrase to politely disagree with their partner's ideas. This is a common way of disagreeing.

<u>Sorry, can I finish?</u>

This student is politely but firmly holding their turn. Turn-taking is an important speaking skill and well worth helping students develop.

A standard text-based lesson procedure

Unit 12: The passive

Pre-reading 1: Work in pairs and discuss the following questions.

■ What items are illegal to bring into your country?
■ Why are these items illegal?
■ What is the punishment for bringing these items into the country?

Pre-reading 2: Read the headline below. Work in pairs. What do you think the police discovered in the luggage?

Police make wild discovery in airport luggage

Reading 1:

Police make wild discovery in airport luggage

A 50-year-old Londoner <u>has been arrested</u> at a UK airport for attempting to bring body parts, bones and eggs from a range of protected species into the country in his luggage. After <u>being stopped and questioned</u> by airport police and customs officials, commercial premises belonging to the man's family <u>were searched</u> and various illegal items <u>were seized</u> and <u>taken away</u> for testing. Amongst a large haul of uncertified items, police found turtle shells and eggs as well as bottles of snake wine, a drink <u>believed</u> to have restorative and curative powers in many parts of Asia.

The smuggled wildlife <u>were listed</u> as endangered by CITES (Convention on International Trade in Endangered Species), and the seized animals <u>will be handed over</u> to the Department of the Environment to establish if they <u>can be returned</u> to their country of origin.

The accused, who claimed the animals were for private collections and gifts, <u>has been released</u> on bail pending further enquiries.

Reading 2: Read the article again and answer the following questions.

1. Where is the man from?
2. Where was he arrested?
3. What species of animals were found in his luggage?
4. What will happen to the animals?
5. What reason did the man give for smuggling the animals?

Grammar 3a: Look at the sentences from the text. Then answer questions 1–4

a. *A 50-year-old Londoner has been arrested.*
b. *Police have arrested a 50-year-old Londoner.*

1. What is the subject of each sentence?
2. In which sentence is the focus on the man? What kind of sentence is this?
3. In which sentence is the focus on the police? What kind of sentence is this?
4. In which sentence can we use 'by' to say who does the action (the agent)?

Grammar 3b: Look at the sentences. Then choose the correct phrase to complete the rule.

a. *Two men from the North of England <u>have been arrested</u> for attempting to bring rare and protected species into the country*
   - We use the passive when the doer (the agent) is known/not known or important/unimportant.

Exercise 1: Put the verbs in the brackets into the correct form using the passive or the active

1. More than 10,000 people _____ (arrest) at UK airports every year.
2. Police _____ (interview) the men for 4 hours.
3. The men's homes _____ (search) but no further evidence _____ (find).
4. The men _____ (claim) that they had bought the animals at a well-known tourist market.
5. The men _____ (release) on bail pending further enquiries.
6. Many endangered animals _____ (sell) for their medicinal properties.

References

Anderson J (2016) Why practice makes perfect sense: The past, present and potential future of the PPP paradigm in language teacher education. *ELT Education and Development* **19**.

Arnold J, Dörnyei Z & Pugliese C (2015) *The Principled Communicative Approach: Seven criteria for success.* London: Helbling.

Austin JL (1962) *How to Do Things with Words.* London: OUP.

Batstone R (2007) *Grammar.* CUP.

Bilborough N (2013) *Memory Activities for Language Learning.* Cambridge: CUP.

Bolitho R (2011) Holistic grammar teaching 3. *ETP* **75**:12–14.

Bolitho R (2015) Language Awareness in Teacher education. *The Teacher Trainer* **29**/1: 2–6.

Borg S & A Burns (2008) Integrating Grammar in Adult TESOL Classrooms. *Applied Linguistics* **29**/3: 456–482.

Brown H (2007) *Principles of Second Language Learning and Teaching.* Pearson Longman.

Brown S (2014) Planning for chaos: a call for realism in teacher training. *IATEFL ESOLSIG Newsletter* **2**.

Carter R, Hughes R & McCarthy M (2011) Telling tails: grammar, the spoken language and materials development. In: B Tomlinson (Ed) *Materials Development in Language Teaching.* Cambridge: CUP.

Chalker S (1994) *Pedagogical Grammar: Principles and problems.*

Claypole M (2011) Bring chaos theory to English language teaching. *The Guardian* **30 July**.

Cook G (1989) *Discourse.* Oxford: OUP.

Council of Europe (2002) *Common European Framework of Reference for Languages: Learning, teaching, assessment.* Cambridge: CUP.

Crystal D (2003) *The Cambridge Encyclopedia of the English Language.* Cambridge: CUP.

Crystal D (2014) Why grammar lessons should be renamed 'understanding language'. *The Guardian Media.*

De Chazal E (2010) Two 'howevers' and 'moreovers' do not a cohesive text make. *IATEFL 2010: Harrogate Conference Selections.*

Dellar H & A Walkley (2016) *Teaching Lexically: Principles and practice.* London: DELTA Publishing.

Dons U (2004) *Descriptive Adequacy of Early Modern English Grammars.* The Hague: Mouton de Gruyter.

Dörnyei Z (2001) *Motivational Strategies in the Language Classroom.* Cambridge: CUP.

Dörnyei Z (2009) Communicative language teaching in the 21st century: The 'principled communicative approach'. *Perspectives* **36**/2: 33–43.

Eales F & S Oakes (2011) *Speakout Upper Intermediate*. Pearson Education.

Eastwood J (2005) *Oxford learners Grammar: Grammar finder*. Oxford: OUP.

Ellis R (2002a) Grammar teaching – practice or consciousness-raising. In: J Richards & W Renandya (Eds) *Methodology in Language Teaching*. Cambridge: CUP.

Ellis R (2002b) The place for grammar instruction in second/foreign language teaching in second language classrooms. In: E Hinkel & S Fotos (Eds) *New Perspectives on Grammar Teaching in Second Language Classrooms*. Oxford: OUP

Ellis R (2003) *Task-based Language Learning and Teaching.* Oxford: OUP.

Ellis R (2008) *The Study of second Language Acquisition* (2nd edn) Oxford: OUP.

Ellis R & N Shintani (2014) *Exploring Language Pedagogy Through Second Language Acquisition Research*. Abingdon: Routledge.

Fernández B & N. Schmitt (2015) How much collocation knowledge do L2 learners have? *International Journal of Applied Linguistics* **166**/1: 94–126.

Field J (2008) *Listening in the Language Classroom*. Cambridge: CUP.

Freeman D (2015) Frozen in thought? How we think and what we do in ELT. *IATEFL Manchester.*

Genette G (1997) *Palimpsests: Literature in the second degre*e. Lincoln, NE: University of Nebraska Press.

Gnutzmann C (2005) 'Standard English' and 'World Standard English': Linguistic and pedagogical considerations. In: Gnutzmann C & F Intemann (Eds) *The Globalisation of English and the English Language Classroom*. Tübingen: Narr.

Hadfield J (1990) *Upper Intermediate Communication Games*. Oxford: OUP.

Hadfield J (2015) Frameworks for creativity in materials design. *IATEFL Conference.* Manchester UK.

Haight C & Herron C & Cole S (2007). The effects of deductive and guided inductive instructional approaches on the learning of grammar in the elementary language college classroom. *Foreign Language Annals*, **40**: 288–309.

Howatt A & R Smith (2014) The history of teaching English as a foreign language: From a British and European perspective. *Language & History,* **57** 1: 75–95.

Huddlestone R & G Pullum (2002) *The Cambridge Grammar of the English Language*. Cambridge: CUP.

Hymes D (1972) On Communicative competence. In: J Pride & J Holmes (Eds) *Sociolinguistics: Selected readings*. Harmondsworth: Penguin.

Kerr P (2014) *Translation and Own-language Activities*. Cambridge: CUP.

Krashen S (1982) *Principles and Practice in Second Language Acquisition*. California: Pergamon.

Lackman K (2016) *Teaching Colligation*. Retrieved from www.kenlackman.com

Larsen-Freeman D (2000) Grammar: Rules, and reasons working together. *ESL/EFL Magazine* 10–12

Larsen-Freeman D (2001) Grammar. In: R Carter and D Nunan (Eds) *The Cambridge Guide to Teaching English to Speakers of Other Languages*. Cambridge: CUP.

Larsen-Freeman D (2003) *Teaching Language*: *From grammar to grammaring*. Boston MA: Heinle.

Larsen-Freeman D (2015) Thinking allowed. Research into practice: Grammar learning and teaching. *Language Teaching* **48**/2: 263–280.

Lewis M (1993) *The Lexical Approach*. Hove: LTP.

Lewis M (2002) *The English Verb*. Boston MA: Heinle.

Lightbown P (1992) Getting quality input in the second/foreign language classroom. In: C Kramsch & S McConnell-Gillett (Eds) *Text and Context: Cross-disciplinary perspectives on language study*. DC Heath & Co.

Littlewood WT (1985) *Integrating the New and the Old in a Communicative Approach.*

Lock G (1996) *Functional English Grammar: An introduction for second language teachers*. Cambridge: CUP.

Loewen S, Li S, Fei F, Thompson A, Nakatsukasa K, Ahn S & Chen X (2009) Second language learners' beliefs about grammar instruction and error correction. *The Modern Language Journal* **93** (1): 9–104.

Long M (1991) Focus on form: A design feature in language teaching methodology. In: K de Bot, R Ginsberg & C Kramsch (Eds) *Foreign Language Research in Cross-Cultural Perspective*. Amsterdam: John Benjamins.

Long M & Norris J (2009) Task-based teaching and assessment. In: K van den Branden, M Bygate & J Norris (Eds) *Task-based Language Teaching: A reader*. Amsterdam: John Benjamins.

Maley A (2011) Squaring the circle – reconciling materials as constraint with materials as empowerment. In: Tomlinson (Ed) *Materials Development in Language Teaching*. Cambridge: CUP.

McCarthy M, O'Keefe A & Walsh S (2010) *Vocabulary Matrix: Understanding, learning, teaching*. Andover: Cengage Learning.

Meier A (2015) The role of noticing in developing intercultural communicative competence. *Eurasian Journal of Applied Linguistics* 25–38.

Mishan F & Timmis I (2015) *Materials Development for TESOL*. Edinburgh: Edinburgh University Press.

Mitchell R (1994) The communicative approach to language teaching: An introduction. In: A Swarbrick (Ed) *Teaching Modern Languages*. London: Routledge.

Murphy R (2012) *English Grammar in Use*. Cambridge: CUP.

Moreillon J (2007) *Collaborative Strategies for Teaching Reading Comprehension: Maximise your impact*. Chicago IL: American Library Association.

Nation P (1996) The Four Strands of a Language Course. *TESOL in Context*. **6** (2): 7–12.

Norrington-Davies D (2015) Leaping before you look. *The Teacher Trainer* **29** (3): 4–7.

Nunan D (1989) *Designing Tasks in the Communicative Classroom*. Cambridge: CUP.

Nunan D (2003) *Practical English Language Teaching*. New York: McGraw Hill.

Parrott M (2010) *Grammar for English Language Teachers*. Cambridge: CUP.

Ortega L (2005) Learner driven attention to form during pre-task planning. In: R Ellis (Ed) *Planning and Task Performance in a Second Language*. Amsterdam: John Benjamins Publishing Company.

Roberts R (2014) Do something different with your course-book. *ETP Issue* **90**: 16–18.

Schmidt R (1990) The role of consciousness in second language learning. *Applied Linguistics* **11** 129–158.

Spada N (2015) SLA Research and L2 Pedagogy: Misapplications and questions of relevance. *Language Teaching* **48** (1): 69–81.

Swain M (1985) Communicative competence: Some roles of comprehensible input and comprehensible output in its development. In: S Gass and C Madden (Eds) *Input in Second Language Acquisition*. Rowley, MA: Newbury House.

Swain M & S Lapkin (1995) Problems in output and the cognitive processes they generate: A step towards second language learning. *Applied Linguistics*. **16**: 371–391.

Swain M & S Lapkin (2008) Lexical learning through a multitask activity: The role of repetition. *Bilingual Education and Bilingualism*. Volume 66: 119.

Swan M (1994) Design criteria for pedagogic language rules. In: Bygate *et al* (Eds) *Grammar and the Language Teacher*. Prentice Hall.

Swan M (2002) Seven Bad Reasons for Teaching Grammar – and two good reasons for teaching some. In: J Richards & W Renendya (Eds) *Methodology in Language Teaching*. Cambridge: CUP.

Swan M (2006) Teaching grammar – does grammar teaching work? *Modern English Teacher*. **15** (2): 5–13.

Swan M (2007) Grammar, meaning and pragmatics: Sorting out the muddle. *TESL-EJ*. **11** (2).

Thompson G (2004) *Introducing Functional Grammar*. London: Hodder Arnold.

Thornbury S (1997a) *About language*. Cambridge: CUP.

Thornbury S (1997b) Reformulation and reconstruction: Tasks that promote 'noticing'. *ELTJ*. **51** (4): 326–335.

Thornbury S (1999) *How to Teach Grammar*. Harlow: Pearson Education.

Thornbury S (2004) Grammar. *ETP*. **32**: 40–41.

Thornbury S (2006) *An A-Z of ELT*. Oxford: Macmillan.

Thornbury S (2015) What do teachers need to know about language? *ETP*. **100**: 9–12.

Tilbury A, L Hendrie, D Rea & T Clementson (2011) *English Unlimited Upper-intermediate*. Cambridge: CUP.

Tomlinson B (2011) *Materials Development in Language Teaching*. Cambridge: CUP.

Ur P (2011) *Active Grammar Teacher's guide*. Cambridge: CUP.

Ur P (2015) Practice and research-based theory in English teacher development. *The European Journal of Applied Linguistics and TEFL*. 143–155.

Widdowson H (1990) *Aspects of Language Teaching*. Oxford: OUP.

Widdowson H (1998) Context, community and Authentic Language. *TESOL Quarterly*. **32** (4): 705-716.

Widdowson H (2003) *Defining Issues in Language Teaching*. Oxford: OUP.

Wilberg P (2010) *One to One: A teacher's handbook*. Brighton: LTP.

Wilkins D (1976) *Notional Syllabuses*. Oxford: OUP.

Williams M & Burden R (1997) *Psychology for Language Teachers*. Cambridge: CUP.

Willis D (2000) Grammar – a textual approach. *ETP* **17**: 5–9.

Willis D (2003) *Rules, Patterns and Words*. Cambridge: CUP.

Willis J (1996) *A Framework for Task-based Learning*. London: Longman.

Willis J & D Willis (2007) *Doing Task-based Teaching*. Oxford: OUP.

Wray A (2002) *Formulaic Language and the Lexicon*. Cambridge: CUP.

Yule G (1998) *Explaining English Grammar*. Oxford: OUP.

Permissions

The author and publisher are grateful to the following who have given permission for the use of copyright material in this book.

'By the time I get to Phoenix' words and music by Jimmy Webb © 1967. Reproduced by permission of EMI Sosaha Music Inc, London W1F 9LD and Sony ATV/Hal Leonard.

'Ed Miliband Labour Housing Pledge' courtesy of Sky News Footage 2015, Sky UK Ltd.

'It's like a drug' reproduced by permission of Speakout Upper Intermediate student's book, Frances Eales & Steve Oakes, Pearson Education 2011.